Scriptural Basis

of the

Divine Liturgy

Scriptural Basis

of the

Divine Liturgy

Meditations on the
Coptic Orthodox Liturgy of Saint Basil

Rany Makaryus

Foreword by Father Antonios Makaryus

Unless otherwise noted, scripture quotations are taken from the New King James Version. © 1982 by Thomas Nelson. Used by permission. All rights reserved.

Other scriptural quotations taken from The Holy Bible, New International Version (NIV). © 1973, 1978, 1984, 2011 by Biblica, Inc.® Used by permission. All rights reserved.

Front cover photo credit: Semon Hanna

Printed in the United States of America
Kindle Direct Publishing

First Edition, 2018

ISBN 978-1-7328918-1-4
ISBN 978-1-7328918-2-1 (e-Book)

Published by Rany Makaryus

This book is dedicated to the loving memory of our
blessed father,

THE VERY REVEREND FATHER YOUHANNA GUIRGIS

Abouna Hanna was greatly devoted to maintaining the
respect and sanctity of the church and the sacraments,
especially the Holy Eucharist.

For as often as you eat this bread and drink this cup,
you proclaim the Lord's death till He comes.

1 Corinthians 11:26

Foreword

The divine liturgy is a spiritual journey that we take on a regular basis. It leads us to receive the Body and Blood of our Lord Jesus Christ, the principal method by which we unite with God. Because it is the heart of worship in our church, it is important for us to realize and understand its elements: where we start, how it ends, and what happens during this incredible journey. Though we may have entered into the physical space of a church, we end up in the heavenly realms, as heaven opens up to us during the prayers of the liturgy. Toward the beginning of this journey, we say that we lift our hearts to heaven, and through the liturgy, this journey that we take, we unite with the heavenly, enter into the very presence of God, and stand before His throne.

We start by asking for forgiveness, not only from God but also from each other, as we extend greetings to one another. Having peace with each other and with God, we then turn our attention to heaven, meditating and reflecting with imagery of the heavenly beings and the throne of God. As we stand before the presence of God, we realize how great a love God must have for us, that He gave so much for our salvation. This leads us to remember the greatest sacrifice given to us by God, which is the sacrifice of His only begotten Son.

During the liturgical prayers, we recall the life of Christ and the sacrifice God made for us to be united with Him. We remember the incarnation of our Lord Jesus Christ, that God became man and subjected Himself to the limitations of being human in all humility for our sake. We remember His passion, His death, and His resurrection from the dead, giving life to us through His victory over death. We also importantly remind ourselves with the Second Coming, in which we eagerly anticipate our ultimate union with God in heaven.

The goal of this spiritual journey is to unify ourselves with Christ. That is why we sometimes call this the sacrament of communion, by which we all have union together in Christ. In this gathering, the whole Body of Christ is received by all the members of the church. All who share in this sacrament attain unity with Christ as one body with many members, together with the heavenly hosts and the saints.

This celebration is the sacrament of sacraments upon which all church sacraments and services are built. It has been passed on to us and preserved through the traditions of the church as an essential part of our faith. This is not only the oldest tradition in the Christian church, but it is also one that has been established for us by Christ Himself. He initiated this tradition for us on the night of the Last Supper when He said to us, "Do this in remembrance of Me" (Lk 22:19). This tradition was taken up by the apostles, who went from house to house breaking bread in unity together, as Christ had taught them.

One way we know that this tradition was handed down from the early church is through the writings of Saint Paul, who said, "For I received from the Lord that which I also delivered to you" (1 Cor 11:23). Though Saint Paul did not receive this tradition from Christ directly, since he was not present at the Last Supper, he did consider that he received it from Christ through the apostles. That same tradition is what he delivered to the early church, and it is the same tradition that we still use to this day in every liturgy we attend.

Impressively, the majority of the prayers in the liturgy have their origins in the scriptures—that is, in the Bible itself. That is why the traditions and prayers of the liturgy have been so well preserved, not only through time but also across different traditions, languages, regions, and cultures. If we strive to understand the meaning behind the prayers used in the liturgy, there is no better way than to go to the core.

By going to the prayer's biblical roots, we can really get a deep and meaningful understanding of them. Furthermore, by participating in this journey regularly, we learn about our faith through the prayers we hear. All of the basic elements and foundations of our faith can be learned through these prayers, which have become a principal way by which the faith is passed on from generation to generation.

This book seeks to identify the many different aspects of this extraordinary journey, why specific prayers are important at certain times of the liturgy, and the biblical basis on which the prayers are formed. Delving into the source of their meaning will help us attain a deeper knowledge of our faith, and we might start to understand the miraculous nature of this great sacrament. This text is a helpful resource for understanding the prayers of the liturgy and why they are so important for the sacrament of the Holy Eucharist.

After reading this, we can have a more accurate understanding of how most of the liturgical prayers are based on biblical references, and have been well preserved, holding true to their biblical origins and the traditions given to us by Christ Himself. It is only by going to the scriptural basis of these prayers that we can gain insight into this spiritual journey of the liturgy.

Foreword by
The Very Reverend Father Antonios Makaryus

Contents

Introduction.................................... 1

Prayer of Reconciliation.......................... 7

The Anaphora.................................. 17

The Institution Narrative........................ 45

The Seven Litanies............................. 63

The Commemoration............................. 81

Introduction to the Fraction..................... 91

The Confession................................. 111

Appendix

Liturgy of Saint Basil with Biblical References... 133

Introduction

The liturgy is an essential part of the life of a Christian. In the Orthodox churches, the sacrament of the Holy Eucharist is considered to be the "sacrament of sacraments." In John 6:56 Christ teaches us, saying, "He who eats My flesh and drinks My blood abides in Me, and I in him." This is how we gain unity with Christ in one body, as Saint Paul describes. Essentially, the Holy Eucharist is the heart of worship in the Orthodox Church and the central core of all church functions. This is not to take away from the importance of other sacraments in the church; however, it is amazing to see that the celebration of the Divine Liturgy is considered to be the core component in the life of a Christian.

All of the sacraments in the church tie into the celebration of the liturgy. First, we note that baptism and confirmation, which are considered essential in the life of a Christian, have a direct connection with the liturgy. New believers cannot immediately partake of the Holy Eucharist; they must first receive the sacraments of baptism and confirmation, before they can receive the Holy Eucharist. The church, however, wastes no time in allowing us to receive the Body and Blood of Christ, as these sacraments are received immediately before the celebration of the Divine Liturgy and the sacrament of the Holy Eucharist. In the case of the sacrament of confession, we are encouraged as believers to repent and confess prior to participating in the liturgy. The sacrament of anointing of the sick also directly relates to the celebration of the liturgy. The sacrament of priesthood, or holy orders, is received in conjunction with the celebration of the liturgy. The sacrament of holy matrimony, although not typically done this way now, is traditionally celebrated as part of the Divine Liturgy. Clearly, with all this, we can see that the church cherishes the sacrament of the Holy Eucharist and often seeks to celebrate this sacrament, either alone or in union with other sacraments.

The depth of meaning behind the words of the liturgy must not be taken for granted, but we should strive to understand their meaning. There is much to gain from simply attending and hearing the prayers of the liturgy besides the fact that we attain unity with God and the body of Christ, which is the church community. The best way to understand this meaning is to go to the source of the words of the liturgy. In fact, the source of most of the phrases of the liturgy is the Bible.

They are not just prayers that some elders of the church came up with at some point, but these prayers have been handed down to us through the traditions of the church and are based on the Bible itself. This is how the liturgy has been preserved throughout hundreds of generations as well as multiple cultures around the world. One clear example of this is seen in the part of liturgy recounting the night our Lord instituted this sacrament.

The words used for this are taken directly from the Bible, and as a result, whether you are attending a Coptic, Armenian, Syriac, Russian, Greek, Roman Catholic, or Lutheran liturgy, you will hear almost exactly the same phrases, word for word.

For example, the Lutheran liturgy uses the following phrase during the segment titled Words of Institution:

> Our Lord Jesus Christ, on the night when
> he was betrayed, took the bread, and when
> he had given thanks, he broke it and gave it
> to his disciples and said: Take; eat; this is my
> body which is given for you.

In the Roman Catholic Mass, the following is said when recalling the breaking of the bread:

The day before He suffered He took break in His sacred hands... He broke the bread, gave it to His disciples and said: Take this, all of you, and eat it, this is My Body, which will be given up for you.

In the Greek Orthodox liturgy, you would hear the following:

He took bread in His holy and pure hands...and breaking it: He gave it to His holy disciples and apostles saying: Take, eat, this is my body which is broken for you and for the forgiveness of sins.

Similarly, in the Russian Orthodox liturgy, you would hear:

Taking bread into His holy and most pure hands...breaking it, He gave it to His holy disciples and apostles, saying: Take, eat: this is my Body which is broken for you, for the remission of sins.

In the Syriac Orthodox Church Anaphora of Saint James, it says:

He took bread into His holy hands...and broke and gave to His holy disciples, and said: Take, eat of it. This is My Body which for you and for many is broken and given for the remission of sins and for eternal life.

In the Armenian Apostolic Church, or Armenian Orthodox Church, the liturgy contains this:

> Taking the bread in his holy, divine, immortal, spotless and creative hands…He broke it and gave it to his chosen, holy disciples, who were seated, saying: Take, eat; this is my body, which is distributed for you and for many, for the expiation and remission of sins.

The Coptic liturgy uses the following phrasing:

> He took bread into His Holy Hands, which are without spot, or blemish…He broke it, and gave it to His own saintly disciples and Holy apostles, saying, "Take, eat of It, all of you, for this is My Body, which is broken for you and for many, to be given for the remission of sins."

These are all current traditions of the churches mentioned above. Notice how the liturgy is preserved between the Oriental and Eastern Orthodox churches, as well as between the Eastern and Western traditions.

This is essentially because of the biblical basis and origin of the liturgy. With the grace of God, this book seeks to understand not only the words of the Coptic liturgy of Saint Basil by going to their Biblical source but also to understand their context in the liturgy.

Prayer of Reconciliation

Whether praying the liturgy of Saint Basil, Saint Gregory, or Saint Cyril, the very first prayer of the liturgy of believers is the prayer of reconciliation. Reconciliation, as defined by Dictionary.com, is "the act of bringing into agreement or harmony; to restore a relationship; to agree to an amicable truce." In this prayer, we recount how God created man without corruption, but then we fell into sin, being tempted by the devil.

God would not allow this to be the end, but he sent his only begotten Son to redeem man from his fall through the greatness of the peace and love he provides us. Therefore, we now have been reunited with God and restored to our original image, as Saint Athanasius describes in his famous literary work *On the Incarnation*.

Why we still maintain an image of corruption is not because of any deficiency on the part of God in our relationship; it is because we have fallen short of the glory of God. Because we stumble, we need constantly to renew our relationship with God, and it is through the liturgy, confessing our sins, and the partaking of the Holy Communion that we can restore this relationship. Hence, before we start the prayers, we remember why we are there and why we need to be active participants in the liturgical service.

"O God, the Great and Eternal..."

The very first phrase of the liturgy, after reading the Word of God through the Epistles, the Acts, and the Gospel, directs our attention to how great God is to His creation. The greatness of God is so awesome that it cannot be fully understood. In Deuteronomy it says, "For the Lord your God is God of gods and Lord of lords, the great God, mighty and awesome" (Dt 10:17). One of the most important attributes of God, making for His greatness, is that He is eternal. Saint Paul reminds Timothy of this when he says, "Now to the King eternal, immortal, invisible, to God who alone is wise, be honor and glory forever and ever" (1 Tm 1:17).

God is not only great, but He is also eternal—that is, without a beginning and without an end. This is such an important statement that the rest of the liturgy is essentially dedicated to grasping the fact that the *great and eternal* God took flesh, the very flesh we would all partake of at the conclusion of the liturgy, in order to grant salvation to His creation. This work of salvation is so amazing and goes way beyond our imagination of greatness.

Looking at those people who are considered great by today's society, it is unfathomable to consider that their greatness was achieved by reducing themselves, whether their greatness is measured by wealth, influence, or other means. The great God, however, has done just that, reduced Himself to the level of His own creation to redeem us and bring us back to the state of incorruption. That is why we start the liturgy by reminding ourselves of the greatness of God, and we sing with David the psalmist, saying, "For the Lord is the great God, and the great King above all gods" (Ps 95:3).

"Who formed man in incorruption and death, which entered into the world through the envy of the devil…"

This quote is taken directly from the book of the Wisdom of Solomon: "For God created man incorruptible, and to the image of His own likeness He made him. But by the envy of the devil, death came into the world: And they follow him that are of his side"(Wisdom 2:23–25 DRA). When humanity was first created, it was given both the *image*, which is immortality and a will based on reason and wisdom, as well as the *likeness*, which is the virtue and holiness, of God.

Humanity existed in incorruption; however, as we realize from this passage, death crept in by the envy of the devil and defiled the image and likeness of God in man. We know that the devil has waged war with God and has targeted humanity, turning God's own creation against the Creator. The devil cannot bear to see glory being offered to God and, being so envious of the happiness and the blessings given to God's creation, therefore deceived the creation and implanted death to destroy humanity.

"You have destroyed by the life-giving manifestation of Your only begotten Son, our Lord, God, and Savior Jesus Christ."

Death entered into the world through Adam's sin, but life is now restored by the resurrection of Christ. Saint Paul clarifies this for us in the epistle to the Romans saying, "For if by the one man's offense death reigned through the one, much more those who receive abundance of grace and of the gift of righteousness will reign in life through the One, Jesus Christ" (Rm 5:17). This entire chapter, Romans 5, describes for us how death entered into the world by Adam's sin; however, the free gift, grace, is now "abounded to many." It is only by Christ's death and resurrection that we were made free from death and given life. This is really a very powerful action based on the strong will of God to save His creation based on love, described by these verses:

For when we were still without strength, in due time Christ died for the ungodly. For scarcely for a righteous man will one die; yet perhaps for a good man someone would even dare to die. But God demonstrates His own love toward us, in that while we were still sinners, Christ died for us. Much more then, having now been justified by His blood, we shall be saved from wrath through Him. (Rom 5:6–9)

This first prayer being offered in the liturgy is a prayer of reconciliation with both God and humanity. We pray that we can have the courage to forgive others around us, realizing that each one of us individually needs the forgiveness of God. We pray that we may once again regain the incorruptible nature God intends for us, His creation. And we realize that this could have only been provided through the incarnation of our Lord; as this chapter in Romans concludes in verse 21, "so that as sin reigned in death, even so grace might reign through righteousness to eternal life through Jesus Christ our Lord."

"You have filled the earth with the heavenly peace, by which the hosts of angels glorify You saying, 'Glory to God in the highest, peace on earth, and goodwill towards men.'"

This is the very familiar phrase we hear during the Christmas season; it is the song the angels sing after the birth of Christ (Lk 2:14). It is most fitting to offer praise through this song, as the Most High God is incarnated and brings heavenly peace to earth. After this, the deacon responds by saying, "Pray for perfect peace, for love, and for the holy apostolic kisses," alluding to the greetings used by the early church and directing the congregants to pray for peace, love, and unity with each other.

"According to your good will, O God, fill our hearts with your peace."

The priest will reiterate this song of the angels by asking that God fill our hearts with peace according to His good will. We know that this peace can only come from God through his goodness. The psalmist says, "You, O God, provided from Your goodness for the poor" (Ps 68:10). We who are poor, in need of God's blessings, love, and peace, must ask God to provide us with the peace of heart we need in order to be able to forgive. Unless we can attain this peace, we would not be able to partake of the holy mysteries.

"Cleanse us from all blemish, all guile, all hypocrisy, all malice, and the remembrance of evil, entailing death."

This prayer is a paraphrasing of the first epistle of Saint Peter, from which we learn that in order "to offer up spiritual sacrifices acceptable to God through Jesus Christ," we must first "[lay] aside all malice, all deceit, hypocrisy, envy, and all evil speaking, as newborn babes, desire the pure milk of the word, that [we] may grow thereby" (1 Pt 2:1–2). When we allow these negative attributes to become part of our lives, we start to distance ourselves from God, we turn away from God, and we start to embrace evil and ultimately death. Instead, here in the liturgy, we pray and ask that God can cleanse us from all this, knowing that we cannot do this on our own. This prayer implies two things: first, that we recognize our faults and our own sins in front of God, and second, that we pray that God forgives us, on the basis that we will in turn forgive those who have wronged us.

"And make us all worthy, O our Master, to greet one another with a holy kiss. That without falling into condemnation, we may partake of Your immortal and heavenly gift, in Christ Jesus, our Lord."

The apostles would send the greetings of Christ through saying this, as Saint Paul says in Romans, "Greet one another with a holy kiss. The churches of Christ greet you" (Rom 16:16). Saint Paul also uses this phrase in the closing of the second book of Corinthians. Again, in 1 Peter 5:14, the last verse of that epistle, we note that

Saint Peter uses a similar phrase, saying, "Greet one another with a kiss of love." The church is made up of a community of believers, and this is noted particularly during the liturgy, where everyone gets together in one spirit, lifting up their hearts and souls to God. It is crucial, therefore, to take a moment during the liturgy to extend the love of Christ to those around us through this greeting. This simple action allows the community as a whole to become unified and be active participants in the prayer.

Furthermore, this is an opportunity for each of us to remember those with whom we may have conflicts and to ask forgiveness. Here we are starting the prayers of the liturgy, and we are about to take part in the miraculous mystery of the Holy Communion; however, before we do that, we need first to examine ourselves and make peace with those around us. In 1 Corinthians 11:27 it says, "Therefore whoever eats this bread or drinks this cup of the Lord in an unworthy manner will be guilty of the body and blood of the Lord." We would not be worthy partakers of this sacrament if we still held resentment and hatred toward our brothers and sisters.

If we are not at peace with one another, then we certainly cannot be at peace with God. Saint John points this out in 1 John 4:20 when he says, "If someone says, 'I love God,' and hates his brother, he is a liar; for he who does not love his brother whom he has seen, how can he love God whom he has not seen?" In order to be at peace with God, we must first make peace with all those around us—those with whom we can interact using all of our senses. If we fail to make peace with each other and reject uniting with each other, then we reject God and the unity we can have with God.

Christ taught us specifically about this when he said, "Therefore, if you are offering your gift at the altar and there remember that your brother or sister has something against you, leave your gift there in front of the altar. First go and be reconciled to them; then come and offer your gift" (Mt 5:23–24). And when we do forgive those around us, we know that God will be inclined to forgive us, as we recall this from praying the Our Father and reading in Matthew 6:14, "For if you forgive men their trespasses, your heavenly Father will also forgive you."

When we approach these sacraments, we must do so with the understanding that we are not perfect. Just as much as we need to have forgiveness from God, we also need to offer forgiveness and ask for it from others. It is at this point that the church community sings together in a unified voice and says, "A mercy of peace, a sacrifice of praise." This is directly a reference to Christ, who is the perfect peace offering, the one who alone can reconcile us with God once more, which is given through the greatness of God's mercy toward us. Hebrews 13:15 says, "Let us continually offer the sacrifice of praise to God, that is, the fruit of *our* lips, giving thanks to His name."

Just as Christ urges us to reconcile with others before we offer our gift on the altar, we remember that in this case, Christ is our sacrifice, the perfect sacrifice of praise, and we must reconcile with others before we take part in this great sacrifice. In fact, this first prayer in the liturgy, the prayer of reconciliation, provides us the opportunity to make peace with each other and continue from there to lift our hearts up to God in prayer, together in one spirit and one mind, unrestrained by any conflicts between members of the body of Christ.

The Anaphora

Upon completing the prayer of reconciliation, the church now considers itself, along with its members, as being in heaven; for this reason we pray, "Lift up your hearts." We have repented before our brothers and sisters, and we have repented before God. Meanwhile, the *Prospharine*, which covers the altar, is removed, signifying the resurrection of Our Lord, through which we receive forgiveness from and union with God.

We notice that the prayers now start to lift our eyes up to heaven, and we start looking upon the angels, the heavenly beings, and all the heavenly powers. There will be a moment when the altar linen coverings will be moved around to symbolize the movement of the angels in heaven. This is the time to close our eyes to the world around us and look through our spirits toward heaven, yearning to become a part and member of the kingdom of God.

"The Lord be with you all."
"And with your spirit."

"The Lord be with you" is the phrase spoken by the Archangel Gabriel to Saint Mary: "Rejoice, highly favored *one*, the Lord *is* with you" (Lk 1:28). This is the greeting we hear from the heavenly, and so this is the greeting that starts the anaphora. This greeting brings peace to our hearts but also instills a sense of fear and trepidation as we approach the holy mysteries of God.

Saint Mary, when she heard this greeting from the angel, was troubled and became fearful. She was not afraid of losing her life or in any kind of danger of physical harm. She feared God and considered this greeting as something she had not deserved. This is a form of reverence to God, understanding His greatness compared to our weakness. We must approach the liturgy and communion with the same fear and reverence, realizing how horribly sinful we are and how greatly forgiving our Lord is to offer us His holy Body as a sacrifice for our sins.

In response to this, the people all reply, saying, "And with your spirit." Saint Paul often used this phrase in his farewell statements closing his epistles. For example, in Galatians 6:18, he says, "Brethren, the grace of our Lord Jesus Christ be with your spirit. Amen." Again in 2

Timothy 4:22 he says, "The Lord Jesus Christ be with your spirit. Grace be with you. Amen." Finally, he also used this phrase in the epistle of Philemon 1:25: "The grace of our Lord Jesus Christ *be* with your spirit. Amen."

In using the words "with your spirit," as opposed to saying "and with you too," this becomes more than just a mere exchange of pleasantries; it becomes a recognition of the spirit of the priest. We realize that through the spirit of the priesthood, God will be performing the miraculous work of changing the bread and wine into the Body and Blood of Christ.

"Lift up your hearts."
"We have them with the Lord."

This phrase comes from the famous passage in the book of Jeremiah the prophet, chapter 3. This passage is read during the twelfth hour of Good Friday, when we remember the burial of Christ. It is during this time when we start to see the beginnings of the change in the expressions of the church, where mourning and repenting of our sins starts to turn into joy and elation as we get closer to the celebrating the Glorious Feast of the Resurrection. In this passage, Jeremiah urges us to repent from our sinful ways and turn back to God. He specifically says:

Let us search out and examine our ways,

> And turn back to the Lord;
> Let us lift our hearts and hands
> To God in heaven. (Jer 3:40–41)

By lifting our hearts up to God, we repent from the evil in our lives and submit ourselves to God, who will provide us forgiveness through His sacrifice on the cross.

"Let us give thanks to the Lord."
"It is meet and right."

The Bible teaches us over and over again to give thanks to the Lord. This is particularly evident in the book of Psalms, where King David takes great joy in expressing his thankfulness to the Lord, encouraging all to do likewise. The famous Psalm 118 starts and ends with this entreaty, saying, "Oh, give thanks to the Lord, for He is good! For His mercy endures forever."

The people all respond to this by saying it is meet and right. As the psalmist also says in Psalm 92:1, "It is good to give thanks to the Lord." Especially during the celebration of the liturgy, as we are about to receive His Body and Blood for the remission of our sins, we are eternally grateful at this opportunity, given our wretched and miserable states. Because we know that we cannot deserve this blessing, and because God has been so gracious to provide us with this blessing regardless of our condition, we express our thankfulness to God for the greatness of his everlasting mercy. Two words used with similar meaning in the Gregorian liturgy are "worthy and just."

Certainly God is worthy of our thanksgiving to Him. In Revelation 4:11, we hear the twenty-four elders saying, "You are worthy, O Lord to receive glory and honor and power." Yes, we have been forgiven from the many sins we have done; however, it is because of how much we have been forgiven that we are so thankful. Just as the sinful woman washed the feet of Jesus with her tears, our Lord said about her that she loved much because she recognized all her sins and was forgiven much. By the same token, if we fail to recognize our sins, we will ask for less forgiveness, and "to whom little is forgiven, the same loves little" (Lk 7:47).

If we find ourselves lacking in thanksgiving to God, who deserves all praise and honor, then we must reevaluate our mind-set at this time and prepare ourselves to be worthy partakers of this sacrament.

Importantly, the idea of giving thanks is very closely tied into the celebration and participation of this sacrament. This sacrament is known as the Holy Eucharist. The word *Eucharist* originates from the Greek word *eucharistia*, which translates as "thanksgiving." This sacrament is—and has been since the very early church—referred to as the Holy Eucharist not only because Christ modeled thanksgiving for us as he instituted this sacrament but also because we are thankful to God for allowing us to receive this sacrament.

"Meet and right, meet and right, truly indeed, it is meet and right. O You, THE BEING, Master, Lord, God of Truth, being before the ages, and reigning forever..."

Here we are reiterating that God is worthy of all glory, honor, and power. In Deuteronomy 32:4 it says, "He is the Rock, His work is perfect; for all His ways are judgment, a God of truth and without iniquity; *just and right is He.*" And in Exodus 15, after the crossing of the Red Sea, as Moses sings his praise to God, he says in verse 18, "The Lord shall *reign forever* and ever." He is the God of Truth, a just God, and "He shall reign forever and ever" (Rv 11:15).

We are trying to describe God and the greatness of His majesty through human understanding and imagery. This is why much of this is difficult to understand; for example, "THE BEING."—God who exists, who existed forever in times past and forever in future times, who existed before anything existed even before the existence of time. Even though it is hard to describe God, we try to understand these aspects of God to lift ourselves into the presence of God, focusing our minds on heaven.

"Who dwells in the highest and looks upon the lowly…"

This is taken directly from Psalm 138:6: "Though the Lord is on high, yet He regards the lowly." This description of God is what resonates with us as Christians. It is the fact that God, who is so great and mighty, would still be concerned with us lowly creatures who have turned against Him and have corrupted His nature in us, bringing evil into the world He created.

We are the lowly ones, the ones for whom God sent His only begotten Son to be given as a ransom for us so that we can regain our union with God. This statement embodies the reason why we celebrate the liturgy, as it is through His regard for the lowly that we can be united with God in Holy Communion.

"Who has created the heaven, the earth, the sea, and all that is therein. The Father of Our Lord, God, and Savior Jesus Christ. By whom You have created all things, visible and invisible."

We are reminded of God as the Creator of all things through Christ, the image of the invisible God. In Colossians 1:16 it says, "For by [Christ] all things were created that are in heaven and that are on earth, visible and invisible…All things were created through Him and for Him." We are recognizing that it is God the Father who has created all things through Our Lord Jesus

Christ, as Saint Paul clarifies here. In this section in Colossians, Saint Paul goes on to say that Christ is the head, the firstborn from the dead, and that he has power and preeminence over all creation. Because of this, it is fitting that all of creation in heaven and earth would be reconciled to God through Christ.

"Who sits upon the throne of His glory; and who is worshiped by all the holy powers…"

The book of Revelation has a great and detailed description of the throne of God in heaven. It is here that we read also about the twenty-four elders and the four living creatures that surround the throne of God,

> Whenever the living creatures give glory and honor and thanks to Him who sits on the throne, who lives forever and ever, the twenty-four elders fall down before Him who sits on the throne and worship Him who lives forever and ever, and cast their crowns before the throne, saying:
> "You are worthy, O Lord,
> To receive glory and honor and power;
> For You created all things,
> And by Your will they exist and
> were created." (Rv 4:9–11)

This is the imagery of heaven that the church hopes to instill in us as we pray the liturgy, guiding us into understanding the greatness of the mysteries that we are participating in. This imagery inspires us to join with the heavenly in praising and worshiping the almighty and all-powerful God, the Pantocrator, who, though he is the Creator of all, has still remembered His creation, even when we have strayed far from Him.

This is when the deacon will reply, "You who are seated, stand." This is a reminder for us that we are in the presence of God, and in reverence, we should stand as we lift our hearts in prayer.

"Before whom stand the angels, the archangels, the principalities, the authorities, the thrones, the dominions, and the powers…"

We, the church, lift our eyes toward God and make note of the surrounding heavenly hosts. From a few verses in Ephesians and Colossians, we can determine five of the nine known ranks of angelic beings:

Seated [Christ] at His right hand in the heavenly *places,* far above all principality and power and might and dominion, and every name that is named, not only in this age but also in that which is to come. (Eph 1:20–21)

> For by Him all things were created…whether thrones or dominions or principalities or powers. (Col 1:16)

From these two texts, we have an overlap of three ranks, namely principalities, powers, and dominions. The other two ranks, thrones and authorities (might), can be added to this, and so we have five ranks of angels from these. In addition to this, we have the angels, the archangels, the cherubim, and the seraphim, all of which have been identified multiple times throughout the Bible. So altogether, there are nine known ranks. This section of the liturgy mentions seven of these ranks, while the cherubim and seraphim are mentioned in the very next section.

Saint John Chrysostom expanded on the phrase seen above from Ephesians, saying, "And every name that is named," and he states that this must mean there are other ranks of angelic beings that are not named or that are known only to God and not yet to us. Regardless, the idea of the liturgy here is to lift us up into heaven, standing among the ranks of angels and looking toward the throne of God.

Importantly, the deacon now replies by saying, "Look toward the east." This is reminiscent of the words of the prophet from Ezekiel 43:2, who says, "And behold, the glory of the God of Israel came from the way of the east. His voice *was* like the sound of many waters; and the earth shone with His glory." Ezekiel here had a vision of the throne of God coming from the east.

It is for this reason that ideally, the churches would be built with the altar facing toward the east, which faces toward the throne of God. In the Gospel of Matthew 24:27, it says, "For as the lightning comes from the east and flashes to the west, so also will the coming of the Son of Man be." The deacon reminding us to look toward the east reminds us of two important points: first, that we should keep our eyes lifted up toward heaven, and second, that we should prepare our hearts to be ready for the Second Coming of our Lord.

"You are He, around whom stand the cherubim full of eyes, and the seraphim with six wings, praising continuously, without ceasing, saying: 'Holy, holy, holy, Lord of Hosts, heaven and earth are full of Your holy glory.'"

This is a direct reference to the heavenly visions seen in the books of Ezekiel, Isaiah, and Revelation. From the book of Ezekiel, specifically in chapter 10, we get a rather detailed description of the cherubim. Here we read a description of them in verse 12: "And their whole body, with their back, their hands, their wings…*were* full of eyes all around." They are further described as having four faces (a cherub, a man, a lion, and an eagle) and wings with the appearance of human hands beneath them, and the sound of their wings could be heard from a great distance. These cherubim stood in the presence of the glory of the Lord.

We find the description of the seraphim in the book of Isaiah, chapter 6. In this chapter, verse 2, we read that the seraphim each "had six wings: with two he covered his face, with two he covered his feet, and with two he flew." They stood above the throne of the Lord, who is described in verse 1 as being "high and lifted up, and the train of His *robe* filled the temple." Furthermore, we read that they cry out one to another, shaking the doorposts by their voices as they say: "Holy, holy, holy *is* the Lord of hosts; The whole earth *is* full of His glory!" (Isaiah 6:3).

Very similarly, in the book of Revelation, we read about the throne room of heaven. The vision here reveals the four living creatures who have some features similar to the cherubim and some like the seraphim. One has the shape of a lion, another of a calf, another of a man, and the fourth has that of an eagle. Like the cherubim described by Ezekiel, they are full of eyes and like the seraphim, they each have six wings, and we read this about them:

> They do not rest day or night, saying:
> "Holy, holy, holy,
> Lord God Almighty,
> Who was and is and is to come!"
> (Rv 4:8)

The cherubim and seraphim are the highest ranks of angels, being in the first class of angels. They are the ones that surround the throne of God. His Holiness the late Pope Shenouda III provides a few points of wisdom in his book *The Angels*. He describes the cherubim as being full of knowledge, as they are full of eyes, with the wisdom to see things from multiple perspectives. Further, we learn about the six wings of the seraphim. They cover their faces with two wings, representing their fear and reverence to the Lord sitting upon His throne. They cover their feet with two wings, representing their humility before God.

Understanding these points, we should remember as we pray during this part of liturgy that we are actually standing in the presence of God, and we need to approach God with reverence and humility, knowing and realizing, even with our limited capabilities, the greatness of the glory of God.

If we pay close attention to what is happening at the altar during this time, we see how the priest moves the linen coverings. Specifically, the two linens used as hand coverings will be switched, and the linen on the chalice will be brought down while one of the other two linens will be brought up to cover the chalice. This movement represents the movements of the cherubim and the seraphim around the heavenly throne. All this happens as we sing the song of the heavenly, saying, "Holy, holy, holy."

"Holy, Holy, Holy, indeed, O Lord our God. Who formed us, created us, and placed us in the paradise of joy. When we disobeyed Your commandment by the deception of the serpent, we fell from eternal life and were exiled from the paradise of joy."

Here the liturgy reiterates the words of the angelic hosts, who do not cease to sing continuously the thrice-holy hymn. It is now that the words of the liturgy start to recount the history of salvation from the fall of Adam and Eve to the death and resurrection of Our Lord Jesus Christ. The beginning of the history of salvation starts with the creation; God, who formed us as pure and innocent humans, placed us in paradise. As the psalmist says in Psalm 139:13, "For You formed my inward parts." God formed us and knows us inside and out. He created everything for humans to enjoy, and in our original innocence, we were deserving of living in paradise so long as we obeyed God.

Ultimately, however, the moment that we strayed from God's ordinances, we could no longer live in paradise, and we were exiled. We could no longer eat from the tree of life, and therefore, for the first time, we faced the punishment of death. This is a summary of the first three chapters in Genesis, which ends in chapter 3, verse 24, saying, "So He drove out the man; and He placed cherubim at the east of the garden of Eden, and a flaming sword which turned every way, to guard the way to the tree of life."

"You have not abandoned us to the end, but have always visited us through Your Holy prophets."

Here there is mention of the history of the Israelites. Though they strayed far from the Lord, He continued to be patient with them and sent prophets to try to bring them back. Our Lord Himself says this in the Gospel: "O Jerusalem, Jerusalem, the one who kills the prophets and stones those who are sent to her! How often I wanted to gather your children together, as a hen gathers her chicks under *her* wings, but you were not willing!" (Mt 23:37).

God continues to seek out and search after those who have strayed away. He tells us through Ezekiel the prophet, "I have no pleasure in the death of the wicked, but that the wicked turn from his way and live" (Ez 33:11). And it is through the Divine Liturgy that we receive the grace of God in the form of the Body and Blood of Christ. It is through this sacrament that we receive forgiveness and ultimately reunite with God and one another, becoming one body.

"And in the last days You manifested Yourself to us, who were sitting in darkness and the shadow of death."

Finally, after the Israelites rejected all the prophets, God revealed Himself to us, as we read in Luke, "Then fear came upon all, and they glorified God, saying, 'A great prophet has risen up among us'; and, 'God has visited His people'" (Lk 7:16). When first visited through the holy prophets, they did not accept God; when visited by our Lord Himself, they still did not accept Him. In fact, our Lord speaks about this in His parable of the wicked vinedressers (Lk 9). In this parable, a vineyard was leased to vinedressers, and the owner was in a far country. He sent multiple servants to get some of the fruit of the vineyard, but they were poorly treated and sent away with nothing. The owner then sent his beloved son, thinking they would respect him; but the vinedressers plotted against his son and killed him, thinking that they would receive his inheritance. Though God knew the evil of this world and what they would do to His Son, Christ still came to deliver the world from our own destruction. Saint Luke records the prophecy of Zacharias after the birth of Saint John the Baptist, stating:

> Through the tender mercy of our God,
> With which the Dayspring from on high has
> visited us;
> To give light to those who sit in darkness
> and the shadow of death,
> To guide our feet into the way of peace.
> (Lk 1:78–79)

Christ came to visit the ones who were sitting in darkness and the shadow of death. He came as a

"Dayspring" to shine his light upon us and guide us "into the way of peace."

"Through Your only begotten Son, our Lord, God, and Savior Jesus Christ, who, of the Holy Spirit and of the Holy Virgin Mary."

In this prayer, we remind ourselves that our Lord, God, and Savior Jesus Christ is not a mere man but is God who was incarnated from the Holy Spirit and from the Virgin Saint Mary. This is what we read and believe from the Gospels. In Matthew 1:18 it says, "Now the birth of Jesus Christ was as follows: After His mother Mary was betrothed to Joseph, before they came together, she was found with child of the Holy Spirit." Furthermore, two verses later, Matthew 1:20 says, "Joseph, son of David, do not be afraid to take to you Mary your wife, for that which is conceived in her is of the Holy Spirit." God sent His only begotten Son to redeem those who would accept Him from evil and death. As we read in John 3:16, "For God so loved the world that He gave His only begotten Son, that whoever believes in Him should not perish but have everlasting life."

God cared so much about the creation that He was willing to become part of the creation—living as a human, with all the physical restraints of a human body, facing the pain and suffering of the death on the cross. Going to the extreme just so that we, who are the pride and joy of God's creation, would return to the original state in which we were created.

"Was incarnate and became man, and taught us the ways of salvation."

At this point, a spoonful of incense is placed in the censer as we remember in our prayers the incarnation. The censer is a symbol of the Virgin Mary, and the incense being placed in the censer is a symbol of the incarnation of our Lord Jesus into her virginal womb. In the Gospel of John 1:14 it says, "And the Word became flesh and dwelt among us, and we beheld His glory, the glory as of the only begotten of the Father, full of grace and truth."

God, who is the Creator, became one of the creation. God, who is unlimited, took on the form of a human with all the limitations that go with it. God, who is immortal, faced the pain of death in the flesh. The one who created time entered into time so that we can be saved from the power of death. God has given us the gift of eternal life and restored us through the incarnation. Saint Athanasius says the following in section 8 of the book *On the Incarnation of the Word*:

> For He did not simply will to become embodied, or will merely to appear...But He takes a body of our kind...And thus taking from our bodies one of like nature,

because all were under penalty of the corruption of death He gave it over to death in the stead of all, and offered it to the Father.

From this, we realize the greatness of the sacrifice that God made for us to have victory over death, to return us to the incorruption that He intended for us, through the grace of the holy resurrection.
It is through the incarnation of our Lord that we have learned the ways of salvation: "Lead me in Your truth and teach me, For You *are* the God of my salvation" (Ps 25:5).

Our Lord teaches us that He is the Way, the Truth, and the Life. He is the path for us to gain salvation. This is salvation from the inevitability of the death we were subjected to when we fell into sin and corrupted the image of God in humans. The life of Christ on earth demonstrates for us the importance of love and sacrifice. Christ demonstrated the greatest love of all when He became the sacrifice offered to God the Father for the salvation of the human race. Symbolically, just like the incense that is placed in the censer, the sweet aroma of His incense was pleasing to God, as read in Ephesians 5:2, "Christ also has loved us and given Himself for us, an offering and a sacrifice to God for a sweet-smelling aroma."

"He granted us the birth from on high through water and Spirit."

Here the liturgy is referring to the sacrament of baptism. It is through this sacrament that the image of God in each of us can be restored to the incorruptible image God intended us to have. When our Lord was describing this birth from on high to Nicodemus, He says, as we read in John 3:5–6, "Most assuredly, I say to you, unless one is born of water and the Spirit, he cannot enter the kingdom of God."

When we are born from the water and the Spirit, we become a new creation. As Saint Paul describes in Colossians 2:12, we were "buried with Him in baptism, in which [we] also were raised with *Him*." Hence, he says in Galatians 2:20, "It is no longer I who live, but Christ lives in me." We have put to death our sinful nature and taken on Christ, and it is through this sacrament that God has granted us again the access to His kingdom.

Saint Peter reiterates this concept in the beginning of his first epistle: "[God] has begotten us again to a living hope through the resurrection of Jesus Christ from the dead, to an inheritance incorruptible and undefiled and that does not fade away, reserved in heaven for you" (1 Pt 1:3–4). Here we see that Saint Peter identifies the inheritance we receive once we have been "begotten again"—in other words, born again, and as Christ tells us, this can only be through the water and the Spirit.

"He made us unto Himself an assembled people, and sanctified us by Your Holy Spirit."

Having been born again, being resurrected with Christ, we now have our citizenship in heaven. When we stand and pray in the liturgy, we are "counted as those standing in heaven"; that is why we are presented with the heavenly vision that leads us to this point from the start of the anaphora. When the liturgy describes us as an assembled people, this is quoted from Hebrews 12:22–23: "But you have come to…the heavenly Jerusalem, to an innumerable company of angels, to the general assembly and church of the firstborn *who are* registered in heaven." We might think of ourselves as an assembled people within the physical church, but this is a much deeper statement.

We are not just gathered with the people around us as we pray at liturgy, but we are gathered with all the heavenly hosts and the assembly of all Christians "who are registered in heaven." This is the greatness of the mystery of the sacrament of communion, that we all become one body in Christ, having one mind and one spirit. Ephesians 4:4 reminds us of this, saying, "There is one body and one Spirit."

We should keep in mind, as we are praying this, that it is only through the grace of God that we are allowed to be members of this great assembly. In 1 Corinthians 6:11, we realize this as we read, "But you were washed, but you were sanctified, but you were justified in the name of the Lord Jesus and by the Spirit of our God." It is only because we have been washed by the Spirit through the waters of baptism and because we have been sanctified by the Spirit of our God that we can be worthy of standing in the presence of the heavenly assembly.

"He loved His own who were in the world, and as a ransom on our behalf, gave Himself up unto death, which reigned over us, whereby we were bound and sold on account of our sins."

In John 13:1 it says that our Lord "loved His own who were in the world, He loved them to the end." Saint John tells us this in his Gospel, as Christ knew that these were his final hours before the crucifixion. Christ willingly gave Himself up to death so that we would not have to suffer the consequences of our sin. Christ became the mediator between God and men:

> For *there is* one God and one Mediator between God and men, *the* Man Christ Jesus, who gave Himself a ransom for all, to be testified in due time. (1 Tm 2:5–6)

He paid for the consequences of our sin. We are the ones who deserved the punishment of death, but Christ is the one who was punished on our behalf. From the history of the fall of man in Genesis, we know that the result of going against the commandments of God is death. This is reiterated in Romans 6:23, but here we also learn that Christ has restored to us the gift of eternal life: "For the wages of sin *is* death, but the gift of God *is* eternal life in Christ Jesus our Lord." We were certainly bound by our sins, just as Saint Peter condemns the sorcerer who tried to purchase the gift of priesthood in Acts 8:32 and said, "For I see that you are poisoned by bitterness and bound by iniquity." This is what David the psalmist speaks about:

> Those who sat in darkness and in the
> shadow of death,
> Bound in affliction and irons—
> Because they rebelled against the words of
> God,
> And despised the counsel of the Most High.
> (Ps 107:10–11)

Death had man bound and sold because of sin, with the wages of that sin being death—death meaning that not only would our life here on earth end but that we would also be bound in Hades thereafter. We "sat in darkness and in the shadow of death" because we broke God's commandment. Without Christ, our condition was certainly miserable.

"He descended into Hades through the cross."

We know that Christ first descended into Hades after His death on the cross. Saint Paul explains this by saying,

> Now this, "He ascended"—what does it mean but that He also first descended into the lower parts of the earth? He who descended is also the One who ascended far above all the heavens, that He might fill all things. (Eph 4:9–10)

By this we understand that Christ first descended into Hades, or the lower parts of the earth, before He ascended into heaven. Saint Peter corroborates this when he speaks of King David's prophesy of the resurrection: "[He] spoke concerning the resurrection of the Christ, that His soul was not left in Hades, nor did His flesh see corruption" (Acts 2:31). Our focus here is that He first descended into Hades upon His death on the cross; however, He was not left in Hades, nor did His body see corruption.

"He rose from the dead on the third day."

It is mentioned in the creed, as well as here in the liturgy, that He rose from the dead on the third day. This time frame is not just based on the calculations of the day Christ was crucified to the day when He rose, but it is based on the scriptures themselves. Christ Himself told us that this would happen through the words of the Gospel; when He was predicting His death and resurrection, He specifically said that He will rise on the third day. This is what the apostles preached, as we read the words of Saint Peter in Acts 10:40, "Him God raised up on the third day, and showed Him openly." In 1 Corinthians 15:4 it says, "He rose again the third day." The resurrection of our Lord is the foundation of Christianity. Saint Paul describes this later in the same chapter by saying, "If Christ is not risen, your faith *is* futile; you are still in your sins!" (1 Cor 15:17). But we know from the eyewitness accounts in the Bible that Christ indeed rose from the dead, and it is through His resurrection that we receive salvation. Saint Paul further explains that point, again in that same chapter, saying, "But now Christ is risen from the dead, *and* has become the firstfruits of those who have fallen asleep" (1 Cor 15:20).

"He ascended into the Heavens and sat at Your Right Hand, O Father."

We read in Mark 16:19 that "He was received up into heaven, and sat down at the right hand of God." There are multiple places where it specifically mentions that Christ is seated at the right hand of God. This is a very important point here, specifically given the words spoken immediately after, talking about the day of judgment.

Christ spoke of this when he was brought in front of the Sanhedrin for judgment: "Hereafter the Son of Man will sit on the right hand of the power of God" (Lk 22:69). The apostles and Saint Paul mention this again multiple times. The significance of this is tremendous. Certainly, God cannot be contained; neither is God limited by a right side and a left side. So this statement of sitting at the right hand of God implies something much deeper and more meaningful.

The right hand of the Father refers to the position of glory and honor. Sitting at the right hand of God can also be understood as Christ being Judge. We read in Revelation, chapter 20, a description of the day of judgment, in which it describes Christ sitting on the great throne. Similarly, when we see someone being brought before a judge, the judge will be seated in the same way that Christ *sits* at the right hand of God, where he is in a position to judge each one of us.

"He has appointed a day for recompense, on which He will appear to judge the world in righteousness, and give each one according to his deeds."

When Saint Paul was preaching to the Athenians, he says that we need to repent, and in Acts 17:31, he goes on to say, "He has appointed a day on which He will judge the world in righteousness." Furthermore, in Romans 2:6, Saint Paul quotes from Psalms and Proverbs, saying that God "will render to each one according to his deeds." A great fear takes over our hearts and minds as we recall the image of Christ sitting on the throne on judgment day.

From the book of Revelation described above, God is reading from the Book of Life, and the dead were judged according to their works. We all know our faults, and we realize how undeserving we are to receive God's grace. We pray that our names are written in the Book of Life, as we learn that anyone whose name is not written there will be thrown into the lake of fire. Here we all pray, asking for God's forgiveness and mercy, saying, "According to Your mercy O Lord, and not according to our sins."

It is only through the grace of God that our names would even be considered for the Book of Life. Without God's mercy, none of us would deserve that honor. This is the work of Christ, through his incarnation, death, and resurrection; He gave us all the gift of eternal life. He rose victorious over death by His resurrection, and in doing so defeated death and restores to us all the gift of life.

The Institution Narrative

We here recall the night of the Last Supper, where our Lord established this sacrament. While doing so, the priest is preparing to handle bread and wine, which is about to become for us the Body and Blood of Christ. Part of this preparation is to *cleanse* his hands using the incense from the censer. This is reminiscent of what happened with Isaiah the prophet as he recounts, "Then one of the seraphim flew to me, having in his hand a live coal *which* he had taken with the tongs from the altar. And he touched my mouth *with it,* and said, 'Behold, this has touched your lips; your iniquity is taken away, and your sin purged'" (Is 6:6–7). This not only symbolizes the cleansing of the hands of the priest, but it also symbolizes the grace we receive through the sacrifice of the only begotten Son of God.

The incense that is placed in the censer, right over the live coal, is sacrificed so that it produces a sweet-smelling aroma. Similarly, our Lord sacrificed His own life for the sake of the whole world and became a sweet-smelling aroma, acceptable to God for the forgiveness of our sins. We are cleansed through His sacrifice for us, and this is the principal reason for the celebration of the liturgy. Here we have reached the essential and most important part of the liturgy, where we remember and follow the way our Lord gave and instituted this sacrament for us.

"He instituted for us this great Mystery of Godliness. For being determined to give Himself up to death for the life of the world."

Christ instituted the Lord's Supper while celebrating the Passover with his disciples on the eve of Good Friday. There are four accounts of this in the Bible, one account in each of the three synoptic Gospels, and one in the First Epistle to the Corinthians. Saint John does not specifically mention this in his Gospel account; however, he describes the circumstances surrounding this, including the teachings Christ imparted to us that evening.

The mystery spoken of here is referenced from 1 Timothy 3:16: "And without controversy great is the mystery of godliness: God was manifested in the flesh, Justified in the Spirit, Seen by angels, Preached among the Gentiles, Believed on in the world, Received up in glory." It is the fact that Christ gives us to eat of His Body that we would have the privilege of uniting with Him through this sacrament. Furthermore, it is the mystery of offering bread and wine, which later becomes for us the Body and the Blood of our Lord Jesus Christ.

"Greater love has no one than this, than to lay down one's life for his friends" (Jn 15:13). Christ showed us the greatness of His love for us when He offered Himself as the sacrificial lamb so that none of us would suffer the consequences of our sin, which is death.

The fact that this was a voluntary decision is very important. Not only was this done willingly but, more importantly, with great determination. In fact, this was the very purpose of the incarnation. As noted in Acts 2:23, Saint Peter, during the sermon he gave on the day of the Pentecost, specifically said, "Him, being delivered by the determined purpose and foreknowledge of God, you have taken by lawless hands, have crucified, and put to death." The capture of our Lord in the garden of Gethsemane, the betrayal by Judas, the trials He faced, and the ultimate crucifixion—these did not happen by chance. God, according to His foreknowledge, knew these events would happen and intended that His only begotten Son would suffer death in the flesh so that He could ultimately defeat death and give us everlasting life.

This is what Christ told us in John 6:33, teaching us that He is the Bread of Life: "For the bread of God is He who comes down from heaven and gives life to the world." This is the very heart of the celebration of the liturgy, the reason why we come together.

"He took bread into His Holy Hands, which are without spot, or blemish, blessed, and Life Giving."

Here the liturgy refers to the fact that Christ is the unblemished lamb offered for the sake of all, as we learn from 1 Peter 1:18–19: "You were not redeemed with corruptible things, *like* silver or gold, from your aimless conduct *received* by tradition from your fathers, but with the precious blood of Christ, as of a lamb without blemish and without spot."

As the perfect lamb, Christ was able to carry our sins and give us the opportunity of being cleansed and purified through the blood He shed for us. It is critical to note the fact that we were not redeemed with corruptible things; no amount of silver or gold can save even one person. Redemption is only possible through the precious Blood of Christ; we were bought at a price, and the ransom paid on our behalf is priceless. It is through this sacrifice that God restored life to us, through the life-giving hands of Christ.

"He looked up toward Heaven to You, O God, who are His Father and Master of everyone. And when He had given thanks. He blessed it. He sanctified it."

Our Lord "broke bread" with his disciples many times over the course of his three years with them. One famous and well-known episode of this is the feeding of the five thousand. In Mark 6:41 it says, "When He had taken the five loaves and the two fish, He looked up to heaven, blessed and broke the loaves, and gave them to His disciples to set before them."

Certainly, we know that Christ had a routine method of breaking bread with his disciples. For example, after the resurrection, Christ appeared and walked with two of the disciples, who were traveling on the road to Emmaus; however, they did not recognize who He was. It was only after they sat to eat dinner that they realized who was with them. This is found in Luke 24:30–31, where it says, "As He sat at the table with them, that He took bread, blessed and broke *it,* and gave it to them. Then their eyes were opened and they knew Him." The fact that they recognized Him by the way in which He broke bread demonstrates that this was based on a routine and methodical fashion that Christ typically used when breaking bread.

As such, we similarly read in all of the synoptic Gospels that as Christ instituted the Lord's Supper, He took bread, blessed and broke it, and gave it to the disciples (Mt 26:26; Mk 14:22; Lk 22:19). Christ's consistent method of breaking the bread was a way to teach the disciples how they should break bread together afterward. This is exactly what still happens during the liturgy today. The priest represents Christ, as it is not the priest but Christ Himself who turns the bread and wine into His Body and Blood. During this time in the liturgy, we see the priest take the bread, look up toward heaven, and say the words that Christ used at the Last Supper, passing on the tradition that was set by the Lord Himself on the evening before His crucifixion.

"He broke it, and gave it to His own saintly disciples and Holy apostles, saying, 'Take, eat of It, all of you, for this is My Body, which is broken for you and for many, to be given for the remission of sins. This do in remembrance of Me.'"

This is taken almost word for word from 1 Corinthians 11:24: "And when He had given thanks, He broke *it* and said, 'Take, eat; this is My body which is broken for you; do this in remembrance of Me.'" This is proof and evidence of the fact that our current traditions in celebrating the liturgy were practiced in a very similar fashion even in the very early days of Christianity. Saint Paul describes the very tradition of celebrating the liturgy in the breaking of bread. He distinctly says in the preceding verse, 1 Corinthians 11:23, "For I received from the Lord that which I also delivered to you." The important thing to see here is that this celebration, instituted by our Lord, is the basis for all Christian gatherings. It is the crux of our beliefs as a Christian community.

"Likewise also, the cup, after supper, He mixed it with wine and water."

The same account of the Last Supper presented in the first book of Corinthians is continued here, where it says, "In the same manner *He* also *took* the cup after supper" (1 Cor 11:25). We say the same phrase during this part of the liturgy—"Likewise also, the cup, after supper"—demonstrating how we hold fast to the traditions given to us from the early church and also showing that the words of the liturgy have a direct biblical basis.

We also see here the teaching from the tradition of our church fathers that the Lord mixed the cup with wine and water. There is great symbolism here, referring to the piercing of our Lord while on the cross after he utters, "It is finished." The Gospel of John 19:33–34 reads, "But one of the soldiers pierced His side with a spear, and immediately blood and water came out."

Saint John Chrysostom, in one of his homilies on Good Friday, points out that the blood and water have a very deep meaning. He informs us that the water is a symbol of baptism and the blood a symbol of the Holy Eucharist. Moreover, he further describes an even deeper meaning. Being that the church is born from these two sacraments, here we see blood and water flowing from Christ's side, symbolizing how the church was fashioned from the side of Christ, just as Eve was fashioned out of Adam's side. This reveals the greatness of the meaning behind the words of the liturgy stating, "He mixed it with wine and water." Though this is not specifically mentioned in biblical texts, certainly the traditions of the church and the teachings of the church fathers reveal this to us (Catechesis of Saint John Chrysostom: Cat. 3, 13–19; SC 50, 174–177).

"And when He had given thanks. He blessed it. He sanctified it. He tasted, and gave It also to His own saintly disciples and Holy apostles, saying, 'Take drink of It all of you, for this is My Blood of the New Covenant, which is shed for you and for many, to be given for the remission of sins. This do in remembrance of Me.'"

Here we continue to recount the words of Christ during the Last Supper, given to us by Saint Paul; however, we also see a stronger reference to the account given in the Gospel of Saint Matthew, where it says, "Then He took the cup, and gave thanks, and gave *it* to them, saying, 'Drink from it, all of you. For this is My blood of the new covenant, which is shed for many for the remission of sins'" (Mt 26:27–28). Again we see how strictly the church has followed the words of Christ Himself at the Last Supper. This is also very close to what is written in 1 Corinthians 11:25: "This cup is the new covenant in My blood. This do, as often as you drink *it,* in remembrance of Me."

We see something very important in both of these accounts. Our Lord was initiating a new tradition that we have now kept for centuries afterward. This is essentially the new covenant that God made with us through the incarnation, death, and resurrection of His only begotten Son and Christ's ultimate victory over death. This victory, this new covenant, is given to us through the Blood of Christ, this very cup that was given to the apostles and that is today given to all of us when we partake of the holy Body and precious Blood of Christ during Holy Communion.

Christ tells us that this cup is the new covenant. This blood that was shed by Christ is the ultimate sacrifice, without which none of us would be able to be reconciled to God. This sacrifice provides forgiveness and remission of our sins and restores us to our original state, being united with God. This is what our Lord says to us in John 6:54–56: "Whoever eats My flesh and drinks My blood has eternal life, and I will raise him up at the last day. For My flesh is food indeed, and My blood is drink indeed. He who eats My flesh and drinks My blood abides in Me, and I in him."

This is the high point of the liturgy where we recall, through the direct words of Christ when he initiated the Last Supper, the very reason why we have gathered together.

"For every time you eat of this bread and drink of this cup, you proclaim My Death, confess My Resurrection, and remember Me till I come."

This is the concluding statement from the account of the events of the Last Supper that Saint Paul gives in 1 Corinthians 11:26: "For as often as you eat this bread and drink this cup, you proclaim the Lord's death till He comes." As seen in the liturgical text here, these words were attributed to our Lord, as if they were spoken by Christ Himself. This is not a very far-fetched notion. First of all, we know that the Bible was written through the guidance and influence of the Holy Spirit. Thus, even though we attribute the writings to a certain author, we know that it is God, through the direction of the Holy Spirit, who gives these authors the words to write. Second, we know that Christ is referred to as the *Logos*, or the Word of God. In this manner, the Bible, which is understood as the Word of God, is given to us as the words God speaks to us directly. Therefore, we can see that Christ Himself is teaching us through the words written by the apostle Paul.

As the church reaches the pinnacle of the liturgy, the congregation sings, "Amen, amen, amen." The word *amen* linguistically originates from Hebrew and means *truth* or *certainty*; it is used by the church to state an emphatic agreement with what is being said and prayed, much like "so be it." We enthusiastically cry out and say, "Your death, O Lord, we proclaim; Your holy resurrection and ascension we confess; we praise You, we bless You, we thank You, O Lord; and we entreat You, O our God."

"Therefore, as we also commemorate His Holy Passion, His Resurrection from the dead, His Ascension into the heavens, His sitting at Your right hand, O Father..."

In celebrating the liturgy and the sacrament of the Holy Eucharist, we are in fact commemorating the passion, death, and resurrection of our Lord Jesus Christ. We call to mind the suffering He went through on our behalf, but more than that, we also realize the victory He gained for us over the slavery of sin and the shackles of death. Our Lord not only resurrected from the dead but also, in so doing, has given life to those who were bound in Hades. He declares this victory by His ascension into heaven and sitting at the right hand of the Father.

Sitting at the right hand of the Father has a great and powerful meaning. Exodus 15:6 says, "Your right hand, O Lord, has become glorious in power; Your right hand, O Lord, has dashed the enemy in pieces." It represents the position of ultimate strength and power; power over our enemies, power over sin, power over the devil, and most obviously here, Christ has demonstrated power over death itself. King David mentions the right hand of God many times, mostly referring to the strength and protection provided by the right hand of God. For example, in Psalm 116:16 he says, "The right hand of the Lord is exalted; the right hand of the Lord does valiantly." Similarly, in the book of Isaiah it says, "The Lord has sworn by His right hand, and by the arm of His strength…" (Is 62:8).

Christ also tells us about His position at the right hand during his trial before the Sanhedrin, where he says, "Hereafter the Son of Man will sit on the right hand of the power of God" (Lk 22:69). Furthermore, Saint Mark witnessed this in his Gospel account and describes the ascension of Christ into the heavens. Specifically, in Mark 16:19 it says, "So then, after the Lord had spoken to them, He was received up into heaven, and sat down at the right hand of God." This was also the vision that was revealed to Saint Stephen, the first martyr, as he was being stoned, leading him to exclaim, "Look! I see the heavens opened and the Son of Man standing at the right hand of God!" (Acts 7:56).

Finally, on this point, we also note what Saint Paul says in Colossians 3:1: "If then you were raised with Christ, seek those things which are above, where Christ is, sitting at the right hand of God." Throughout our lives, and particularly during the liturgy, we ought to be seeking those things that are above. Very often in our lives we turn to God regarding our earthly needs; however, we are being reminded to turn to God first and foremost for our spiritual needs, for the forgiveness of our sins, and for eternal life given though the Body and Blood of Christ.

"And His Second Coming from the heavens, awesome and full of glory…"

During the liturgy, our minds are directed toward the heavenly gifts given to us by God. As we turn our attention to attaining eternal life with God, we are also reminded about the Second Coming of Christ. Perhaps no book is more direct and forthright about the Second Coming of Christ as the Epistles to the Thessalonians. In these epistles, Saint Paul encourages us through the imagery of the Second Coming of our Lord Jesus Christ. In 1 Thessalonians 4:16–17 we read, "For the Lord Himself will descend from heaven with a shout, with the voice of an archangel, and with the trumpet of God. And the dead in Christ will rise first. Then we who are alive *and* remain shall be caught up together with them in the clouds to meet the Lord in the air. And thus we shall always be with the Lord." This is what we should be seeking as we prepare ourselves to partake from this holy sacrament.

"We offer unto You Your gifts from what is Yours…"

This phrase, "we offer unto You Your gifts from what is Yours," has a very deep and profound meaning.

Here we are saying that we have offered this bread and wine to God. First, these gifts have been given to us from God Himself, as we do not have anything that is from ourselves, but all that we have is from God. Second, these gifts, which are in and of themselves gifts from God, are being offered back to God as gifts from us. Finally, and most importantly, we should stress that we specifically say "Your gifts." This is because we are following what our Lord Himself did on the night He instituted this sacrament, where Christ offered bread and wine, which were then changed into His Body and Blood. Similarly, this is what Melchizedek offered at the time of Abraham, as we read in Genesis 14:18: "Then Melchizedek king of Salem brought out bread and wine." This is why David says in the Psalms,

> The Lord has sworn
> And will not relent,
> "You *are* a priest forever
> According to the order of Melchizedek."
> (Ps 110:4)

This is explained to us in the book of Hebrews, where Melchizedek is described as "without father, without mother, without genealogy, having neither beginning of days nor end of life, but made like the Son of God, remains a priest continually" (Heb 7:3). Melchizedek, whose name is translated to mean "king of righteousness" and is noted to be the king of Salem—

meaning the king of peace—is a prototype of Christ, a manifestation of God in the Old Testament. Therefore, the bread and wine offered during the liturgy are God's gifts, and that is why we say "Your gifts."

"For everything, concerning everything, and in everything…"

This is very similar to what is prayed in the thanksgiving prayer, "we thank You for everything, concerning everything, and in everything." The offering of our prayers in the liturgy do not depend on how well the church community is doing, how large or small a congregation is, or even how prosperous the church is. This concept also applies for each of us—we should be actively participating in the liturgy, no matter what is going on in our lives. These prayers, these gifts of bread and wine, are offered no matter the situation. Saint Paul says in 1 Thessalonians 5:16–18, "Rejoice always, pray without ceasing, in everything give thanks; for this is the will of God in Christ Jesus for you." We should be looking forward to being in liturgy, participating in the liturgical prayers, and being united together as one body in Christ through communion.

It is easy and simple to follow this when everything in our lives is going well, when we are not worried about everything collapsing around us, when we feel that we are in control. However, we are taught that we should pray without ceasing, no matter what the situation is, and that we should be thankful for all the good times and the bad. Taking that one step further, we should not just be thankful, but we should be joyful and rejoice. How could we attain such an optimistic, enthusiastic, and joyous outlook on life? If we could easily answer that, then many of the problems we face on a daily basis would be resolved.

The fact is, this is not easy to do, but we do get further instruction on this in Philippians 4:11–12: "For I have learned in whatever state I am, to be content: I know how to be abased, and I know how to abound. Everywhere and in all things I have learned both to be full and to be hungry, both to abound and to suffer need." We learn from this that there is one key factor we should strive for, and that is to be content in whatever state we are in. When we find ourselves content with little, we will find that God will continue to provide for us the things we need, though not necessarily the things we desire. Through contentment, even when having little, we will find it easy to offer gifts to God in any situation, whether out of abundance or despite suffering need.

The church again remembers to pray, saying, "We praise You, we bless You, we serve You, we worship You."

"And this bread He makes into His Holy Body. And this cup also, the Precious Blood of His New Covenant."

This is when the priest prays for the descent of the Holy Spirit on the offered gifts, the bread and the wine. It is when these words are uttered that the gifts on the altar will become the Body and the Blood of our Lord. It is important to point out a couple important items here. First, we must understand to whom the pronouns in these statements are referring. The pronoun *He* in the statement, "And this bread He makes into His Holy Body," refers to God the Holy Spirit, and *His* in that same statement refers to God the Son, who is our Lord Jesus Christ.

These pronouns are clearly understood this way when we note that the entire liturgy of Saint Basil is directed to God the Father; therefore, if the liturgy was to mention a pronoun to refer to God the Father, the pronoun *You* would be used. The same statement in the Gregorian liturgy, which is directed to God the Son, saying, "And this bread He makes into Your Holy Body" further corroborates this. Note here that the pronoun *He* is referring to God the Holy Spirit, while the pronoun *You* is referring to God the Son. Here, then, it is clear that the mystery of this sacrament is performed through the work of the Holy Spirit by the use of the pronoun *He*.

Second, we note that the priest would sign the cross over the bread three times before finishing the first word of the phrase, "And this bread He makes into His Holy Body." Similarly, for the chalice, the priest would sign the Cross over the cup three times before finishing the first word of the phrase, "And this cup also, the Precious Blood of His New Covenant." This is because once the bread is transformed into the Body of Christ, it would be improper to sign the Cross over it, and similarly for the wine once it has become the Blood of Christ. After this part of the liturgy, the priest would no longer sign the Cross over himself or the people, as the blessings are directly proceeding from the Body and Blood of Christ on the altar.

The Seven Litanies

Christ tells us in Matthew 18:20 that "for where two or three are gathered together in My Name, I am there in the midst of them." We understand that God is truly present with us in spirit whenever we gather together in prayer. Now that the Body and Blood of Christ are on the altar, the church takes this opportunity to offer supplications to God, who is truly present with us, not only in spirit but also in flesh, through His only begotten Son, Jesus Christ. We bring our supplications to God, asking for His mercy and grace to grow in the church and the church members.

"Make us all worthy, O our Master, to partake of Your Holies, unto the purification of souls, bodies, and our spirits..."

Again here we bring to mind the words of Saint Paul in 1 Corinthians 11:27: "Therefore whoever eats this bread or drinks *this* cup of the Lord in an unworthy manner will be guilty of the body and blood of the Lord." Yet we realize and understand that we cannot be worthy of this, no matter what we do, but it is only through the grace of God that we can be made worthy to partake of this sacrament. So we are led in prayer immediately after the sanctification of the gifts of bread and wine, where they become the Body and Blood of Christ, to ask God that we would be made worthy of such a blessing, that we would be worthy of receiving Christ and becoming one with Him. Hence we pray that we would be purified in soul, body, and spirit.

Ironically, it is only through the Blood of Christ that we can be purified, and this is why we constantly need to partake of this sacrament. In Hebrews 9:13–14 it says, "For if the blood of bulls and goats and the ashes of a heifer, sprinkling the unclean, sanctifies for the purifying of the flesh, how much more shall the blood of Christ, who through the eternal Spirit offered Himself without spot to God, cleanse your conscience from dead works to serve the living God?" We understand from this that we are purified through Christ, who cleanses us from sin and death. In Colossians 1:12 it says, "Giving thanks to the Father who has qualified us to be partakers of the inheritance of the saints in the light."

"That we may become one body and one spirit…"

This is the result of being purified through this sacrament. We each partake of the Body and Blood of Christ, and as a result, we become members of one body in Christ and have communion with one another. This is the main goal of this sacrament in the church, that we would always act in unison and harmony, with each member growing stronger to strengthen the community of believers as a whole. This is what Saint Paul teaches us in 1 Corinthians 12, immediately after he talks about breaking the bread when everyone comes together as a church.

He explains that there certainly are many gifts, but the same Spirit; multiple ministries, but the same Lord; and multiple works, but the same God who works in everyone. He says specifically in verse 12, "For as the body is one and has many members, but all the members of that one body, being many, are one body, so also *is* Christ." Therefore, if we have each received the Body of Christ, we cannot be divided among ourselves but rather are united in Christ. This is why he goes on to say in verses 13 and 14, "For by one Spirit we were all baptized into one body…and have all been made to drink into one Spirit. For in fact the body is not one member but many."

Similarly, the apostles held a deeper understanding of the meaning of using only one bread for celebrating the Holy Eucharist. Through their teachings in the Didache, we understand the importance of having one bread, as it says in section IX–4, "As this broken bread was scattered upon the mountains, but was brought together [the wheat harvested, sifted and ground] and became one, so let thy Church be gathered together from the ends of the earth into thy kingdom." Just as the ingredients for the bread were scattered across the earth before they came together to make the one bread, so also are all of us. We are scattered across the earth, but we all come together into body through this sacrament. This is one of the most essential and important concepts of celebrating the liturgy.

"And may have a share and inheritance with all the saints who have pleased You since the beginning."

The liturgy now is starting to focus our attention on the promises of God that we receive and the blessings we gain from receiving the Body and Blood of Christ. That is another reason why we start with these seven short litanies, as they represent the promises of God that we receive whenever we ask for anything in the name of Christ. We start by asking and praying that we would first be made worthy to partake of this sacrament and furthermore that this sacrament would purify us and that we would all become one body in Christ, that we would all have part of the share of the inheritance God has promised us.

We read about this promise in Hebrews 9:15: "And for this reason He is the Mediator of the new covenant, by means of death, for the redemption of the transgressions under the first covenant, that those who are called may receive the promise of the eternal inheritance." God has certainly promised this inheritance of eternal life for those who receive this sacrament.

Remember that in John 14:3–4, our Lord told the disciples before He was crucified, "I go to prepare a place for you. And if I go and prepare a place for you, I will come again and receive you to Myself; that where I am, there you may be also." God has an inheritance waiting for us, a share that He is preparing for us so that we can be with Him. Saint Peter, in his first epistle, explicitly states this, as he says that "our Lord Jesus Christ, who according to His abundant mercy has begotten us again to a living hope through the resurrection of Jesus Christ from the dead, to an inheritance incorruptible and undefiled and that does not fade away, reserved in heaven for you" (1 Pt 1:3). This is from the abundance of love that God has for each one of us.

We then should be grateful and thankful for His mercy and grace that allow us as sinners to become worthy of this inheritance, as Saint Paul prays in Colossians 1:12 that we would always be "giving thanks to the Father who has qualified us to be partakers of the inheritance of the saints in the light."

"Remember, O Lord, the peace of Your One, Only, Holy, catholic, and Apostolic Church."

The very first supplication we make here to God is that we keep the peace and unity in the church. This is essential to the celebration of the liturgy and participation in communion. Any divisions, any altercations, any factions within the church can take away from this spirit of unity in Christ and nullify the blessings that we receive in this sacrament. That is why the liturgy starts with the prayer of reconciliation; this is why false teachings and divisive language are not tolerated in the church.

There is no room for pride or self-gloating, as our primary focus is on the message of the Risen Christ. For this reason much time and effort is spent on unifying the church, at least in dogma, not only within Orthodoxy but across all sects of Christianity. It is this basic and common faith that binds us together; as we read in Romans 5:1, "Therefore, having been justified by faith, we have peace with God through our Lord Jesus Christ." It is through this sacrament of receiving Christ that we are able to have peace with God. "And the peace of God, which surpasses all understanding, will guard your hearts and minds through Christ Jesus" (Phil 4:7).

"This, which You have acquired to Yourself with the Precious Blood of Your Christ, keep her in peace, with all the Orthodox Bishops who are in her. Foremost remember, O Lord, our blessed and honored father, the archbishop, our patriarch, and

his partner in the [apostolic] liturgy, our father the Bishop."

Our second supplication is that God would help and support the patriarch and bishops, who are the leaders of the church. We notice here that we are reminded of how important the church is to God, as we say that this church was purchased as a very high cost, which was through the Blood of our Lord Jesus Christ. This, as we have mentioned earlier, is taken from 1 Peter 1:19, where we learn that we have been redeemed "with the precious blood of Christ, as of a lamb without blemish and without spot." In fact, Saint John Chrysostom paints the picture for us to always remember this by saying, "As God then took a rib from Adam's side to fashion a woman, so Christ has given us blood and water from his side to fashion the Church." This church, which God has purchased through the shedding of the blood of His only begotten Son, must be so precious to Him, and we are praying that He would guide the leaders of the church so that we would not lose this precious jewel God has entrusted to be in their hands, through the guidance of the Holy Spirit.

"And those who rightly handle the Word of Truth with him, grant them unto Your Holy Church to shepherd Your flock in peace. Remember, O Lord, the Orthodox Hegomens, Priests, and deacons."

We continue this line of supplications in this third prayer we make, where we similarly pray for the leaders of the local churches to be guided by the Holy Spirit in their work as well. The work of the elders of the church is very important and should not be taken lightly, as we can see that the church is very valuable to God. This is why Saint Paul says to Timothy, "Be diligent to present yourself approved to God, a worker who does not need to be ashamed, rightly dividing the word of truth" (2 Tm 2:15). Similarly, in Acts we see that he gives a similar message to the elders of the church in Ephesus, saying, "Therefore take heed to yourselves and to all the flock, among which the Holy Spirit has made you overseers, to shepherd the church of God which He purchased with His own blood" (Acts 20:28). Saint Peter also delivers this message in his first epistle, where he says,

> The elders who are among you I exhort, I who am a fellow elder and a witness of the sufferings of Christ, and also a partaker of the glory that will be revealed: Shepherd the flock of God which is among you, serving as overseers, not by compulsion but willingly, not for dishonest gain but eagerly; nor as being lords over those entrusted to you, but being examples to the flock; and when the Chief Shepherd appears, you will receive the crown of glory that does not fade away. (1 Pt 5:1–4)

We can see how seriously he took his mission of shepherding the flock of God, the very mission that Christ delivered to him directly on the day Christ restored him after the denial, found in John 21:15–19. Christ commands Saint Peter each time he says, "You know that I love you," saying, "Feed My lambs," "Tend My sheep," and "Feed My sheep." This he certainly took to heart and put into practice throughout the rest of his life. Remembering that the true Shepherd, who is Christ, will return to give blessings to those who fulfill this command.

"And all the servants, all who are in virginity, and the purity of all Your faithful people. Remember, O Lord, to have mercy upon us all."

In this fourth prayer, we ask that God would have mercy on all His people. We are the precious church that God has acquired unto Himself; we are the reason why God sent His only begotten Son. We are asking that God would preserve us in Him. Saint Peter tells us how important we all are, that we have now become so special in the eyes of God:

> But you are a chosen generation, a royal
> priesthood, a holy nation, His own special
> people, that you may proclaim the praises of
> Him who called you out of darkness into
> His marvelous light; who once *were* not a

people but *are* now the people of God, who had not obtained mercy but now have obtained mercy. (1 Pt 2:9–10)

We should always remember that we have not been able to deserve the grace we have been given; however, it is only from God that we have been given the blessing of being His chosen people. We know that God has had much mercy on us, as we pray in Psalm 130:7, "O Israel, hope in the Lord; for with the Lord there is mercy, and with Him is abundant redemption." That is why the whole church cries out at this time, saying, "Have mercy upon us, O God, the Father the Pantocrator."

"Remember, O Lord, the salvation of this, Your Holy place, and every place, and every monastery of our Orthodox Fathers."

The fifth supplication that we make is that we would be able to live in safety and that all the dwellings of the faithful would be protected by God. We know that God is the one who protects us and guards us throughout our lives. In the Psalms we pray the following:

> I will both lie down in peace, and sleep;
> For You alone, O Lord, make me dwell in
> safety.
> (Ps 4:8)

As much as we may have assurances of safety in our daily lives, we know that ultimately, God is the one who protects us in any given situation. Of course, that is not to say that we should not be safe in how we manage our lives, but we should pray that while we do our part, God would protect us.

"And those who dwell therein in God's faith. Graciously accord, O Lord, to bless the air of heaven, the fruits of the earth, the waters of the river, the seeds, the herbs, and the plants of the field this year."

In Ephesians 3:17 we read, "That Christ may dwell in your hearts through faith." When Christ lives within us, we prosper. In Genesis 39:2 it says, "The Lord was with Joseph, and he was a successful man." Certainly, God provides for us those things we need and gives blessings to those who follow Him, according to His wisdom. David says in Psalm 122:7, "Peace be within your walls, prosperity within your palaces." We learn that there are blessings promised to those who return to God, as we read in Deuteronomy 30:5: "[God] will prosper you and multiply you more than your fathers." Saint John, in the second verse of his third epistle, says, "Beloved, I pray that you may prosper in all things and be in health, just as your soul prospers." Certainly God loves to see his children become successful and gives to us according to our abilities. In the sixth of these supplications, we ask that God would bless the work we do and give prosperity to the land that is being cultivated.

"Raise them to their measure according to Your Grace. Give joy to the face of the earth. May its furrows be abundantly watered and its fruits be plentiful. Prepare it for sowing and harvesting. Manage our lives as deemed fit. Bless the crown of the year with Your goodness..."

In Ephesians 4:7 we read, "But to each one of us grace was given according to the measure of Christ's gift." God gives to each of us according to His grace. Not all of us have the same gifts and abilities; however, whatever gifts we have, we should use. As Saint Paul says again in Romans 12:6, "Having then gifts differing according to the grace that is given to us, let us use them." Here we pray that according to His grace and according to His measure, we ask that God would bless what has been given to us to the maximum potential—not for selfish ambitions and desires but so we would be able to really impact those around us for the glory of the kingdom of God. We ask God to provide for us the tools we need to carry out His plan, and we pray for prosperity in our land. As David says in the Psalms,

You send forth Your Spirit, they are created;
And You renew the face of the earth.
(Ps 104:30)

God provides all the tools we need to be able to carry out the plan He has for us:

You water its ridges abundantly,
You settle its furrows;
You make it soft with showers,
You bless its growth.
You crown the year with Your goodness,
And Your paths drip with abundance.
(Ps 65:10–11)

Again here we see that the words used in the liturgical service are mostly based on the Bible. These prayers offered in this way are, in a sense, reminding God of his promises to us and are holding Him accountable for fulfilling His promises. We do this based on His saying that whatever we ask in His name, He will give to us.

"For the sake of the poor of Your people, the widow, the orphan, the traveler, the stranger, and for the sake of us all who entreat You and seek Your Holy Name. For the eyes of everyone wait upon You, for You give them their food in due season."

As we ask for abundance in the gifts God provides for us, we also remember those who are the most vulnerable in our communities. We remember that as a community, as one body, when one member suffers, the whole body will suffer as well. That is why we pray especially for the widows, the orphans, the travelers, and the strangers. Those are the ones among us who may feel the most anxiety, who have no one to look out for them, and who can be easily forgotten and lost in the community. This is why, in the tradition of the early churches, something that stemmed from the early Jewish traditions, these specific groups of people are considered the ones who need the most help.

When talking about works of mercy, these are the people who would first come to mind. It is important to realize that we not only pray for these people but that we should also be energized through this prayer to go and search for these people and really help them, making sure they are not suffering silently in need. Though we may be the messengers of God in providing assistance to others around us, we know that ultimately, however, it is God who provides:

> The Lord upholds all who fall,
> And raises up all who are bowed down.
> The eyes of all look expectantly to You,
> And You give them their food in due season.
> (Ps 145:14–16)

These all wait for You,
That You may give them their food in due
season.
(Ps 104:27)

God is the true source of all sustenance for us, and we should not take this for granted. It is part of the blessings He gives to us according to His grace.

"Deal with us according to Your goodness, O You who give food to all flesh. Fill our hearts with joy and gladness, that we too, having sufficiency in everything always, may abound in every good deed."

We pray that God would provide for us according to His goodness and not according to our sinfulness. If it were based on our actions, we would not have deserved any of the things we have received; however, it is because of the love that God has and His goodness that we have been blessed with so much in our lives:

Who gives food to all flesh,
For His mercy endures forever.
(Ps 136:25)

This is one of the psalms we use for the midnight praises every day in the fourth canticle.

Furthermore, we also remember the words of Saint Paul in Acts 14:17, where he was faced with the idolatry at Lystra and said, "Nevertheless He did not leave Himself without witness, in that He did good, gave us rain from heaven and fruitful seasons, filling our hearts with food and gladness." And it was again Saint Paul who said in 2 Corinthians 9:8, "And God *is* able to make all grace abound toward you, that you, always having all sufficiency in all things, may have an abundance for every good work."

This is our prayer here, that as we make these petitions to Christ, we believe based on our relationship and experience with God that He will provide for us all that we need. Therefore, to sum up our petitions, we remind ourselves that God works through us, and as He has provided for us through those around us, so we also should provide for our brothers in need through good works to them.

"Remember, O Lord, those who brought to You these gifts, those on whose behalf they have been brought, and those by whom they have been brought. Give them all the Heavenly reward."

This is the last of the seven litanies prayed at this time of the liturgy. We should pay close attention to the word *remember*, as it is used multiple times in these prayers. For example, in this prayer, when we are asking the Lord to *remember* the ones who have brought these gifts, we should be certain that God does not forget anyone. Christ reassured this by saying, "Are not five sparrows sold for two copper coins? And not one of them is forgotten before God…Do not fear therefore, you are of more value than many sparrows" (Lk 12:6–7). Our God is all knowing and, therefore, He cannot and will not forget us. So then why do we pray saying, "Remember, O Lord"?

There is a famous prayer request made by the thief who was crucified with Christ. We repeat this prayer throughout the Lenten season, and also it is prayed multiple times at the sixth hour of Good Friday as we remember the crucifixion. It says,

> Lord, remember me when You come into
> Your kingdom. (Lk 23:42)

When we feel that God has forgotten us, it is very likely that we have forgotten, ignored, and abandoned God. In this prayer, we are asking God to help us turn back to Him, to accept our repentance, and to grant us the gift of salvation. In essence, we are praying that God would accept us into His holy kingdom. In this context, *remember* is not meant to bring back a memory that may have been forgotten, but it is meant to ask God to have mercy on us when we stand before Him on Judgment Day.

This idea relates very closely to the conclusion of this prayer, where we ask that God provide those who have offered these gifts to receive the "Heavenly reward." The church, being thankful to those who have offered these gifts, prays that they would receive the heavenly reward. Christ expounds on this when He teaches us how to perform charitable deeds toward one another. He says, "Take heed that you do not do your charitable deeds before men, to be seen by them. Otherwise you have no reward from your Father in heaven" (Mt 6:1). He goes on to teach us that we should not do our good deeds in hopes of gaining glory from men, but we should keep them secret, knowing that God will give us the heavenly reward.

The Commemoration

The commemoration of the saints is an important part of liturgy that has been handed down to us from the early church traditions. In fact, across all early traditions of the church, no matter if you were in Antioch, Rome, Alexandria, or any other Christian region, the liturgy always included the commemoration of the saints. Saint Augustine of Hippo makes note of the importance of this by saying, "Neither are the souls of the pious dead separated from the Church which even now is the kingdom of Christ. Otherwise there would be no remembrance of them at the altar of God in the communication of the Body of Christ" (*The City of God* 20:9:2, AD 419).

This rings true from our reading of Romans 8:35–39, where we are asked, "Who shall separate us from the love of Christ?" It goes on from there to say that neither death nor life can separate us from the love of God. We can understand from this passage that we are united in the love of Christ, and therefore, death cannot separate us from this unity. This is why the church insists on remembering the saints and those who have departed in the love of Christ. Similarly, Saint Gregory of Nyssa spoke of Ephraim the Syrian, saying, "You who are standing at the divine altar [in heaven]…bear us all in remembrance, petitioning for us the remission of sins, and the fruition of an everlasting kingdom" (*Sermon on Ephraim the Syrian*, AD 380).

In the early part of the liturgy, specifically in the anaphora, we focus on the heavenly beings, the angels and the heavenly orders; by commemorating the saints, we again lift ourselves up to heaven. This is a symbol of our respect for our elders, as Saint Peter describes:

> Likewise you younger people, submit yourselves to *your* elders. Yes, all of *you* be submissive to one another, and be clothed with humility, for God resists the proud, But gives grace to the humble. (1 Pt 5:5)

In the liturgy, we are humbled by the presence of the saints all around us, as is written in Hebrews 12:1: "Therefore we also, since we are surrounded by so great a cloud of witnesses, let us lay aside every weight, and the sin which so easily ensnares *us*, and let us run with endurance the race that is set before us…" Here we are encouraged to run the race with strength and endurance, being surrounded by this cloud of witnesses, who are the saints that have finished their race and now can give us encouragement to complete ours. Of course, the ultimate and true example for us is Christ Himself, who we look toward and who all the saints are aspiring to emulate.

"As this, O Lord, is the command of Your Only Begotten Son, that we share in the commemoration of Your saints…"

Saint Basil has asserted here in the liturgy that the commemoration of the saints is a command of the only begotten Son. Hebrews 13:7 explicitly says, "Remember those who rule over you, who have spoken the word of God to you, whose faith follow, considering the outcome of *their* conduct." We are commanded to remember the saints who have "spoken the word of God" to us, who we know have achieved the heavenly reward for their strife and as a result of their conduct. Similarly, we are commanded to give special honor to our elders, "Let the elders who rule well be counted worthy of double honor, especially those who labor in the word and doctrine" (1 Tm 5:17).

Our Lord gives us an example of this when He spoke highly of the woman who had anointed Him with the costly fragrant oil. When her actions were questioned, Christ immediately came to her defense and said that she will be commemorated for her bravery and belief in

Him. Specifically, He said, "Assuredly, I say to you, wherever this gospel is preached in the whole world, what this woman has done will also be told as a memorial to her" (Mt 26:13). See here that He says, "What this woman has done"—this good deed will become her memorial. Certainly, there is no question that Christ is encouraging us to remember the saints, not merely to honor them but more importantly to become more like them in what we do. It should also be emphasized that we are not praying to the saints or asking them for forgiveness, but rather we ask for the prayers of the saints, who can intercede before God for us; yet it is through Christ and the grace of God that we can obtain mercy.

We must further understand that the Bible clearly is our reference for the truth; however, when there are questions, we look toward the early church fathers, their writing, and their interpretations of the scriptures. As a true Apostolic church, we consider both of these together, the Bible and the teachings of the early church fathers, to comprise the basic elements of our Orthodox Christian dogma and beliefs. Some may question whether Christ Himself has given this command to us, as there is no direct quote in the Bible that attributes to our Lord the spoken word where Jesus commands us to remember the saints directly. We did see above, however, the example of the woman who anointed Christ and how He spoke of the memorial to her. We also see above the command given to us in the book of

Hebrews, where we are commanded to remember the saints.

We should keep in mind that Christ is the *Logos* of the Father, or the Word of God. God inspires all scripture, though written by man, and the Bible is the Word of God; therefore, to us, what is written in the Bible is the message given to us by God directly. Furthermore, the sayings of the early fathers, such as Saint Basil, give us deeper insights to our beliefs. This well known saying of St. Basil, as it is used in liturgy here, is one of the reasons why the church encourages us to commemorate the saints.

"Graciously accord, O Lord, to remember all the saints who have pleased You since the beginning: our Holy fathers the patriarchs, the prophets, the apostles, the preachers, the evangelists, the martyrs, and the confessors and all the spirits of the righteous perfected in the faith."

Before we start mentioning the names of saints in the commemoration, we start by mentioning the categories of the saints. While it would be great to remember all the saints individually, that is not practical at every liturgy; therefore, the categories of the saints are remembered first, reminding us that there are many more saints than those mentioned. By bringing that to our attention, we realize that we are counting ourselves as standing in heaven before the throne of God, standing

among the saints whom we are calling upon, as is
described in Hebrews:

> But you have come to Mount Zion and to
> the city of the living God, the heavenly
> Jerusalem, to an innumerable company of
> angels, to the general assembly and church
> of the firstborn who are registered in
> heaven, to God the Judge of all, to the
> spirits of just men made perfect, to Jesus the
> Mediator of the new covenant. (Heb 12:22–
> 24)

This is heavenly Jerusalem, a place we hope to reach
and look forward to be, along with the saints who have
great faith that was made perfect through their works.
Just as was described in James 2:22, "Do you see that
faith was working together with his works, and by works
faith was made perfect?" These saints we mention are
clear examples of those who have shown their faith by
their works. From here we start to mention the names
of individual saints, starting, of course, with the most
holy Saint Mary, who is the mother of our Lord and
Savior, followed by Saint John the Baptist, Saint
Stephen, and then Saint Mark, who is the founder of the
church in Egypt and the first bishop of Alexandria. This
is followed by multiple other bishops and patriarchs of
the early church, including Saint John Chrysostom, Saint
Basil, Saint Cyril, and Saint Gregory, who are each

liturgical authors. From there we go on to mention the elders who were present at the three ecumenical councils at Nicaea, Constantinople, and Ephesus, followed by Saint Anthony and the Desert Fathers.

Some also choose to mention modern-day saints, such as recently departed bishops and patriarchs who have been canonized. The church continuously generates saints throughout all times, even in this present day. The point here is not to mention the names of all these great saints of the church, but it is important to understand the spirit of the unity we have with the saints, who are in heaven praying for us.

"And all the choir of Your saints, through whose prayers and supplications, have mercy on us all, and save us, for the sake of Your Holy Name, which is called upon us."

After mentioning the names of all the saints, we ask them to pray for us and intercede to God our Father, who stands in our presence. We humble ourselves before these saints, recognizing that they have a much more intimate relationship with God, and ask that God would hear our prayers through their pleadings for us. Of course, as God loves each and every one of us and rejoices and celebrates at the return of a sinner, we know that our prayers offered to God are heard before we even utter them. It is, however, in the spirit of humility and unity with the body of Christ that we ask this. In the Psalms, we pray with David:

> Not unto us, O Lord, not unto us,
> But to Your name give glory,
> Because of Your mercy,
> Because of Your truth.
> (Ps 115:1)

We are asking for mercy based on the name on which we are called. That name called upon us Christians is Christ, and it is only through the saving grace given to us by our Savior Jesus Christ that we are able to attain mercy and unity with God and the saints:

> If My people who are called by My name will humble themselves, and pray and seek My face, and turn from their wicked ways, then I will hear from heaven, and will forgive their sin and heal their land. Now My eyes will be open and My ears attentive to prayer made in this place. (2 Chr 7:14–15)

At this point the deacon responds by saying that the readers will remember the names of all the patriarchs who have fallen asleep, starting with Saint Mark, the first Pope and Patriarch of Alexandria. The church congregation then responds by singing the following:

"May their holy blessings be with us. Amen.
Glory to You, O Lord. Lord have mercy.
Lord bless us. Lord repose them. Amen."

Introduction to the Fraction

At this point in the liturgy, we present three important prayers before God. First, we ask and pray for all the souls of those who have departed to be accepted into the heavenly kingdom, as we have just remembered the names of all the saints who have preceded us. Second, we pray for ourselves as we continue our journey to heaven, asking for peace in this difficult voyage. Third, we pray and give thanks that God has given us this opportunity to be counted among the saints in heaven as we come together in preparation for receiving Holy Communion. We notice that these prayers all focus on heaven. Starting from our entry into the church, where we are greeted with icons of Christ and many of the saints, and continuing to the prayers throughout the liturgy, our attention is constantly redirected toward heaven.

Participating in the sacrament of Holy Communion unites us with the heavenly, and the church as a whole is lifted up. It becomes a holy place, a part of heaven, and as a result, we then are standing in heaven. What is heaven without the presence of God, and at this point in the liturgy, with the presence of Christ on the altar, how can we describe the church but as a true extension of heaven? This is why it is crucial that we stand, kneel, and bow down with great reverence to God, who is present with us. Movements are kept to a minimum, talking is limited only to the prayers being made, we turn away from any of the distractions, and we focus all our attention on God.

"Those, O Lord, whose souls You have taken, repose them in the paradise of joy, in the region of the living forever, in the Heavenly Jerusalem in that place."

Here we see that the fathers equate the heavenly Jerusalem, which is mentioned in Hebrews 12, with paradise, the place of the living forever. This is what was spoken of by Saint Paul in 1 Thessalonians 4:17: "Then we who are alive *and* remain shall be caught up together with them in the clouds to meet the Lord in the air. And thus we shall always be with the Lord." This eternal life is what Christ speaks about in John 6:51 and 6:54, when He says, "I am the living bread which came down from heaven. If anyone eats of this bread, he will live forever…Whoever eats My flesh and drinks My blood has eternal life." Those who are living forever are the ones who have followed Christ, received the Body and Blood of Christ, suffered in this world for the sake of Christ, and now have been eternally united with Him in the heavenly Jerusalem. This power over death was achieved through the victory of our Lord over death and through His glorious resurrection. That is why in Revelation 1:18 we read these words spoken by Christ: "I *am* He who lives, and was dead, and behold, I am alive forevermore." As Christ died in the flesh, He conquered death, and through His resurrection we are given victory with Him over death.

One important phrase used here is the mention of the paradise of joy. We have now heard this term repeated in the liturgy a few times, and it refers to the Garden of Eden in the book of Genesis. In fact, looking at the etymology of the word *Eden*, we realize that it comes from the ancient Hebrew term that means "pleasure" or "delight." The term *paradise of joy* is common to the early church, and the roots can be found in the Septuagint translation of the Bible. The Septuagint was the early translation of the Old Testament scripture in the third century BCE into Koine Greek. The term *Koine Greek*, meaning "common Greek," refers to the language spoken throughout the Mediterranean region following the conquest of Alexander the Great. This was done by seventy-two scholars, hence the term *Septuagint* and the abbreviation LXX, referring to the number seventy. The literal translation of the term *Garden of Eden* is translated as "paradise of joy" or "garden of delight." When the church fathers reference the paradise of joy, we are not being encouraged to seek a material paradise, but a heavenly and spiritual abode with God.

"And we too, who are sojourners in this place, keep us in Your faith, and grant us Your peace unto the end."

As we are approaching the time of communion, when we would be united with Christ, we realize that our time here on earth is limited, while our time in heaven will be eternal. This is why the liturgy uses the phrase *sojourners in this place*. This is what David says in his praise in 1 Chronicles 29:15: "For we are aliens and pilgrims before You, as were all our fathers; our days on earth are as a shadow." We should always keep in mind this fact, that our life here on earth is but a shadow, and we are here as though we are pilgrims or sojourners. If we constantly recognize this throughout our lives, we would be much more likely to keep our minds focused on eternal life in heaven, and as a result, we would tailor our lives toward reaching that goal.

Saint Paul refers to this heavenly goal in Hebrews. After he mentions the faith of Abel, Enoch, Noah, Abraham, and Sarah, he says that they had "died in faith…and confessed that they were strangers and pilgrims on the earth. For those who say such things declare plainly that they seek a homeland" (Heb 11:13–14). He is explaining how the use of such a phrase—"strangers and pilgrims on the earth"—indicates that they are looking forward to something else, to returning to their homeland. Importantly stated here is that they "died in faith." Hence, we pray here that God would help keep us in His faith, the same faith that Abraham kept, the faith that God would bring us safely to our heavenly destination. Furthermore, in 1 Peter 2:11, Saint Peter urges us to be honorable in our actions during this journey: "Beloved, I beg you as sojourners and pilgrims, abstain from fleshly lusts which war against the soul." Clearly, he is stating that our life here on earth is simply a journey. It is our soul that will live on, and our bodies are only the vehicle for this journey. If we are to focus on the vehicle only, then we neglect the goal of our journey—reaching our homeland, which is heaven.

As soon as we pray for our journey through this life on earth, we start to focus on the eternal. We forget the temporal life, full of pain and struggle, and focus on life in His kingdom, free of suffering, free of misery, free of sin, and full of peace. We remember the words of Christ in John 14:27: "Peace I leave with you, My peace I give to you; not as the world gives do I give to you. Let not your heart be troubled, neither let it be afraid." If we direct all our energy and focus on the journey—that is, our life on earth—then fear can easily overtake us; however, it is only when we focus on God and our heavenly destination that peace can fill our lives. Saint

Paul explicitly states this in Romans 8:6, saying, "For to be carnally minded *is* death, but to be spiritually minded *is* life and peace." We pray that the "peace of God, which surpasses all understanding will guard [our] hearts and minds through Christ Jesus" (Phil 4:7). It is only through Christ and the sacrifice made for us that we can receive this peace, and so the congregation prays together, saying, "As it was in the beginning…" (Christ was in the beginning with God, per John 1:1) and continues now that we have been given new life through Him and will always be, from generation to generation, and to the end of ages. This praise mimics that which was written in the letter to the Ephesians: "To Him *be* glory in the church by Christ Jesus to all generations, forever and ever. Amen" (Eph 3:21).

"Lead us throughout the way into Your kingdom, that as in this, so also in all things, Your Great and Holy Name may be Glorified, Blessed and exalted in everything, Honored and Blessed with Jesus Christ, Your Beloved Son, and the Holy Spirit. Peace be with all."

We have now shifted our focus to heaven, where we have faith we will one day be united with God. As we get closer to the time of communion, we start to realize the reality of this amazing promise God has given us. Here we pray that God would lead us to our final destination, that He would be our guide throughout our journey. Notice that we pray for God to lead us all "throughout the way," not just to get us to the destination.

We know that the journey will be filled with challenges, and if we hope to get through them, we acknowledge that we will need God to guide us. Christ told us, "Narrow is the gate and difficult is the way that leads to life" (Mt 7:14). If we think we can get through this journey alone, we are quite mistaken; it is only by the grace of God that we would be able to find the way into God's kingdom. In 2 Corinthians 2:14 it says, "Now thanks be to God who always leads us in triumph in Christ." We know that Christ Himself is "the Way" to reach the kingdom of God (Jn 14:6); He is the one who leads us in triumph. This is the sole purpose for our gathering during liturgy, that through receiving the Bread of Life, the Body of Christ, we would be led by God throughout our life on earth into His kingdom. In Psalms, David prays for God to lead him through the difficulties he faces:

> Teach me Your way, O Lord,
> And lead me in a smooth path, because of
> my enemies.
> (Ps 27:11)

> And see if *there is any* wicked way in me,
> And lead me in the way everlasting.
> (Ps 139:24)

He is praying that God would redirect him from his wicked ways and lead him to the way toward everlasting life in heaven. God also revealed to Isaiah His desire to lead us and clearly tells us that He is the one who should teach us the way, saying, "I *am* the Lord your God, Who teaches you to profit, Who leads you by the way you should go" (Is 48:17). Without this guidance, we would be completely lost, but with God leading the way, there is no concern over where we will end up. This is why when Christ called on the disciples to follow Him, they immediately left everything and did just that—they followed Him.

There is, however, a major caveat to this: essentially, following Christ is not going to be easy. Christ describes this in Matthew 16:24, saying, "If anyone desires to come after Me, let him deny himself, and take up his cross, and follow Me." Note the key steps in this instruction. First, we should desire to follow Christ; second, we should deny ourselves; third, we must carry our cross; finally, we then can follow Him. This seems to be a rather difficult process, especially when our faith is weak; however, if we trust God and accept His grace, He will increase our desire to follow Him, self-denial will be easy to accept, and God will guide us and help us as we carry our cross.

One important aspect to consider is the motivating force behind our desire to follow God. In Psalm 23:3 we read, "He leads me in the paths of righteousness for His name's sake." Again in Psalm 31:3 we read, "For You *are* my rock and my fortress; therefore, for Your name's sake, lead me and guide me." Here it becomes apparent that the reason God leads us is for His name's sake. Another way to look at it is that we follow God for the sake of His name; this is much more obvious in Isaiah 63:14, where he says, "You lead Your people, to make Yourself a glorious name." The reason we ask God to lead us is so that we can demonstrate the greatness of God and to glorify His name. Saint Paul speaks of this in his second letter to the Thessalonians, saying, "Therefore we also pray always for you…that the name of our Lord Jesus Christ may be glorified in you, and you in Him, according to the grace of our God and the Lord Jesus Christ" (2 Thes 1:12). This is similarly stated in the liturgy: "So that as in this, so also in all things, Your great and Holy Name be glorified." The reality is that the kingdom of God grows, and His name is honored and glorified as more of us are led and guided by Him.

"Again, let us give thanks to God the Pantocrator, the Father of our Lord, God, and Savior Jesus Christ."

Here at the remembrance of the holy name of God, we remember to give thanks for the greatness of the love God has demonstrated to us. David, who was always full of thanksgiving and praise, mentions this multiple times:

Sing praise to the Lord, you saints of His,

And give thanks at the remembrance of His
holy name.
(Ps 30:4)

Rejoice in the Lord, you righteous,
And give thanks at the remembrance of His
holy name.
(Ps 97:12)

To give thanks to Your holy name,
To triumph in Your praise.
(1 Chr 16:35)

David understood how awesome is the name of
God, and he did not even get to see the fulfillment of
the story of redemption. How much more should we
give thanks at the remembrance of the name of our Lord
and Savior Jesus Christ, who gave Himself for us?
Philippians 2:9–11 says, "Therefore God also has highly
exalted Him and given Him the name which is above
every name, that at the name of Jesus every knee should
bow, of those in heaven, and of those on earth, and of
those under the earth." We give thanks to God for giving
us His only begotten Son, for redeeming us and granting
us salvation even though we are the ones who turned
away from Him; we give thanks to God for returning us
back to the original image we were created in through
the passion, death, and resurrection of Christ, whose
Body and Blood we receive during communion.

"For He also has made us worthy now to stand in this Holy Place, to lift up our hands and to serve His Holy Name."

During this part of liturgy, we are thanking God for making us worthy of all the blessings we are receiving. If we turn to 2 Thessalonians 1:11, we can see this more clearly: "Therefore we also pray always for you that our God would count you worthy of *this* calling, and fulfill all the good pleasure of *His* goodness and the work of faith with power." This is a great honor that we are receiving, and we must recognize its greatness.

We are not worthy by our own means, but it is God who has made us worthy. Again we can remember the verse in Colossians 1:12 that describes "giving thanks to the Father who has qualified us to be partakers of the inheritance of the saints in the light." God has qualified us and made us worthy of this great and blessed honor. Specifically, we are thankful for being made worthy of three things: first, "to stand in this holy place"; second, "to lift up our hands"; and third, "to serve His Holy Name."

First, we are thankful that we are worthy to stand in the church, in the holy place, in the sanctuary among all the saints we have mentioned earlier. We are reminded of what God told Moses the great prophet when he went to look at the bush that was burning but not being consumed. God spoke to him in Exodus 3:5 and said, "Do not draw near this place. Take your sandals off your feet, for the place where you stand *is* holy ground." Moses was so reverent that he hid his face from God. We should also approach this sacrament, this celebration of the liturgy, our receiving of the Body and Blood of Christ with high reverence. We should not be distracted with our minds wandering about, unfocused, not realizing the amazing gift we are receiving. In Psalm 24:3 David asks, "Who may ascend into the hill of the Lord? Or who may stand in His holy place?" Certainly, we are not worthy to do so, but we give thanks that God has allowed us to be worthy of this. Christ reminds us to pray that we would be able to stand before Him, telling us in Luke 21:36 to watch and pray: "Watch therefore, and pray always that you may be counted worthy to escape all these things that will come to pass, and to stand before the Son of Man."

Second, we are also thankful that God has allowed us to be worthy of lifting our hands up in prayer. David commands us to lift our hands up to God in prayer; in Psalm 63:4 we read, "Thus I will bless You while I live; I will lift up my hands in Your name." Again in Psalm 134:2 he says, "Lift up your hands *in* the sanctuary, And bless the Lord." Not only does he command us to lift our hands up to God, but he also prays that God would accept the lifting of our hands as an acceptable sacrifice. In Psalm 141:2 he says, "Let my prayer be set before You *as* incense, The lifting up of my hands *as* the evening sacrifice." He is asking that our prayers be received before God as he receives the sacrifices offered—our prayers as incense and the lifting of our hands as the offered sacrifice.

Finally, we also thank God for making us worthy "to serve His Holy Name." The great Saint Paul, who preached and spread God's word throughout many cities, never forgot his former evils as a blasphemer and persecutor of the church and speaks of this in his first epistle to Timothy: "And I thank Christ Jesus our Lord who has enabled me, because He counted me faithful, putting *me* into the ministry" (1 Tm 1:12). The service we offer in God's name is not to be taken lightly, but we should count it as a great honor; we are blessed with this great gift of being part of the work God has set out to do. God used the gifts Saint Paul had to do His work, and He continues to use the gifts each of us has to advance His kingdom.

We should count ourselves as fortunate to be part of this awesome and amazing work. This mindset of the apostles and the saints should be the attitude of those who serve in the church. God has granted that we would be part of His great work; this is what God spoke to the prophet Jeremiah: "If you repent, I will restore you that you may serve me" (Jer 15:19, NIV). We thank God for the greatness of His grace, in which we are allowed to be a part of His great work and serve Him.

"Let us also ask Him to make us worthy of the communion and partaking of His Divine and Immortal Mysteries."

While anticipating the blessing we are about to receive in Holy Communion, we remember all the blessings we have already received. This is why we give thanks (as we have discussed in the preceding prayers). We give thanks that God has allowed us to partake in this blessed event. We thank God for making us worthy to stand, lift our hands, and serve Him. Additionally, we ask and pray that God would make us worthy to receive this sacrament. This is very much a reiteration of what was prayed earlier in the beginning of the seven short prayers: "Make us all worthy, O our Master, to partake of Your holies…" To recapitulate that discussion, we remind ourselves of the verse in 1 Corinthians 11:27, which says, "Therefore whoever eats this bread or drinks *this* cup of the Lord in an unworthy manner will be guilty of the body and blood of the Lord." All the while we realize that we are purified only through the Blood of Christ, who cleanses us from sin and death.

"The Holy Body. And the Precious Blood."

At this time, the priest holds up the bread that has become the body of Christ and declares this by saying, "The Holy Body"; meanwhile the entire congregation bows down in worship, saying, "We worship Your Holy Body." And after this, the priest takes one finger and dips it into the cup, saying, "And the Precious Blood," and again the congregation responds by saying, "We also worship the Precious Blood." During this time, the priest then takes the finger that was just dipped into the cup and touches the Body with it, drawing a line with the Blood in the shape of a cross. This action indicates that this Blood belongs to this Body, and as we can see in the very next section, it is proclaimed that these belong to Christ.

"Of His Christ, the Pantocrator, the Lord Our God. Peace be with all."

As the priest identifies that this Body and this Blood belong to Christ, it is further declared that Christ is the Pantocrator. At this point, the deacon calls out to everyone to pray fervently, reminding us that we should all be praying that God would allow us to be worthy of receiving this great sacrament. As we are remembering our unworthy state, the church together prays: "Lord have mercy." So as not to make us dwell in fear of our sins and possibly question if we should even approach these "Immortal Mysteries," we are reminded of the peace of God, "which surpasses all understanding." We cannot fully understand the love God has for us, where He would allow us sinners to be worthy of becoming united with Him who is perfect through this sacrament of communion.

Here in particular we see the term *Pantocrator* to describe Christ. All throughout this liturgical prayer, which is directed to God the Father, the term *Pantocrator* is used to describe God the Father. *Pantocrator* comes from the Greek Septuagint translation of the Bible. In fact, the word *Pantocrator* was used to translate both of the following titles used for God in the Old Testament, "Lord of Hosts" or "Yahweh Sabaoth" and "God Almighty" or "El Shaddai." As previously described, the Septuagint was completed in the third century BCE; therefore, it does not include New Testament books.

The New Testament, however, did not need to be translated into Koine Greek, as the original language for the books of the New Testament was Greek. The term *Pantocrator* was not limited to use in the Old Testament but was also used in the New Testament, though not very frequently. Besides only one mention in the Pauline Epistles, the only other book to use *Pantocrator* is the book of Revelation, where it appears multiple times. Certainly, there is no question that the letters to the Corinthians were written in Greek, as the primary language of the intended audience was Greek. Therefore, we know that in 1 Corinthians 6:18, Saint Paul directly uses the term *Pantocrator* in reference to God, as he quotes 2 Samuel 7:14 in the Septuagint, saying, "I will be a Father to you, and you shall be My sons and daughters, says the Lord Almighty." Here the Hebrew translation of "Almighty" is "El Shaddai" and the Greek translation is "Pantocrator." Saint John, in the book of Revelation, refers to God as the Pantocrator nine times, identifying God as almighty and omnipotent. The fact that here in the liturgy we identify Christ as the Pantocrator is really a declaration that Christ is God. He is one with the Father and the Holy Spirit, inseparable, equal, and of one essence; Christ, with the Father and the Holy Spirit, make the Holy Trinity, one God.

The Fraction

The fraction is a seasonal prayer that is selected based on the liturgical calendar. Though any fraction prayer can be prayed at any time of the year, these prayers typically coincide with the season the church is celebrating, or it may coincide with the feast of a saint commemorated on that day. There are multiple options for this prayer, including an annual prayer, a fraction prayed during the Advent season, others prayed during the Lenten season, one that is used at the feast of the Resurrection and for the fifty days afterward, one that is prayed during and preceding the feast of Saint Mary and any feasts of heavenly beings, as well as many other fraction prayers.

The reason this prayer is called the fraction is because it is when the Body is divided, or fractioned. This is the breaking of the bread, as it was referred to at the time of the apostles. For example, in Acts it says, "And they continued steadfastly in the apostles' doctrine and fellowship, in the breaking of bread, and in prayers" (Acts 2:42). The fraction is performed in a very specific way so that twelve pieces surround the center piece, called the *spadikon*. This center piece symbolizes Christ, and the twelve pieces around it symbolize the twelve apostles surrounding Christ.

At the end of the fraction, we are directed to pray using the very prayer that Christ taught us, Our Father. This prayer can be found in the Gospels of Matthew and Luke. The Lord gives us this prayer as the prototypical prayer we ought to use. There is so much that can be said about this prayer, which goes way beyond the scope of this book; however, a few observations regarding this prayer are significant in the context of the liturgy. First, this prayer is directed to God the Father, as are the rest of the prayers of this liturgy. Second, we note the use of the possessive pronoun: *our*. This is very important, as it implies that although we are all individuals, we are all praying together as one unit. Specifically, that is the one body that is united together though Christ in the sacrament of Holy Communion. Finally, in this prayer, we are asking God to provide us with "our daily bread." This has multiple meanings, but the most important meaning in this context is Christ as the Bread of Life. In John 6:35 we read, "And Jesus said to them, 'I am the bread of life. He who comes to Me shall never hunger, and he who believes in Me shall never thirst.'"

Our Lord teaches us a very important lesson regarding bread for sustenance. He said that we should not focus on food that does not last, but we should instead focus on the food that leads to eternal life. This is none other than the Body and Blood of our Lord. This is the focal point of these liturgical prayers, "our daily bread" that is Christ, the Bread of Life. Interestingly, the concept of forgiveness ties directly into this, as the very next part of this prayer leads us to ask for forgiveness, as we forgive others. The unity that we achieve with each other in the liturgy is directly related to the forgiveness we all receive from God through the sacrificial offering of His only begotten Son, our Lord, God, and Savior Jesus Christ.

The Confession

This is the final prayer before we approach the altar and receive the sacrament of Holy Communion. It is at this point that we all declare and confess our belief that this really is the actual Body and Blood of Christ. We declare our faith that the bread and wine we have just offered to God are no longer bread and wine but now are in fact the Body and Blood of Emmanuel our God. We must be certain of our faith in this before we approach this great mystery. Before we sing with the rest of the congregation and say, "Amen, I believe," we need to ask ourselves if we really do believe. This is not something easy; in fact, it is very difficult to perceive or understand. Believing that this is the true Body and Blood of Christ requires a great amount of faith. We should all pray at this time that God would give the faith needed to believe.

"The Holies for the holy. Blessed be the Lord Jesus Christ the Son of God; the sanctification is by the Holy Spirit. Amen."

The statement made here is a strong reminder for all of us before we approach and receive the Body and Blood of Christ. It is declared that the "Holies" are for the "holy." The "Holies" is in reference to the mystery of the Body and Blood of Christ on the altar, and the "holy" refers to the congregants who are gathered in the church and waiting to receive the sacrament. Saint Peter reminds us of the command written in the book of Leviticus, saying, "Be holy, for I am holy" (1 Pt 1:16). We are called to be holy; we are called to be set apart for God. The word *holy* means to be separated apart and dedicated to God. This is reminiscent of the prayer Christ prayed for His disciples and His church before the crucifixion, recorded in the Gospel of John:

> The world has hated them because they are not of the world, just as I am not of the world. I do not pray that You should take them out of the world, but that You should keep them from the evil one. They are not of the world, just as I am not of the world. Sanctify them by Your truth. Your word is truth. As You sent Me into the world, I also have sent them into the world. And for their

sakes I sanctify Myself, that they also may
be sanctified by the truth. (Jn 17:14–19)

Christ is praying for our sanctification, for our holiness, as He teaches us that we are not of this world though we are in the world. The famous example of this is a boat in the middle of the ocean. Those who are onboard are in the ocean, though they are not from the ocean. They are set apart from the ocean waters beneath and the wildlife of the ocean waters through the safety of the boat. In the same way, we are in this world though we do not belong to this world; we are protected and sanctified by God.

Saint Paul reminds us many times that we are called to be saints, and he mentions the saints of the various churches as he wrote his epistles. He recognized that we have all been called to be sanctified, and as a result, we are set apart as holy for God. This brings on many thoughts and questions of true worthiness. Are we worthy of being called saints? Have we been set apart from this world? Are we indeed holy—can these "Holies" be meant for us?

Just as this statement is declared, there is a true sense of fear and reverence for the sacrament we are gathered together to receive. The fact is that we are not holy because of anything we have done, but it is through Christ that we have become holy, that we are considered saints through Him. Just as Christ said in this prayer above, "For their sakes I sanctify Myself, that they also may be sanctified by the truth." We are reminded that only those who are holy should receive communion, but we learn that it is only through the sacrifice of Christ that we have been made holy.

There is no question that, in and of ourselves, we are not worthy of this blessed sacrament, but for anyone to deny themselves from receiving this sacrament because they are not worthy is a great deception. The reality is that Christ has redeemed us by His Blood, and we have been washed by the Blood of Christ through the holy waters of baptism. This is clearly stated in Revelation 1:5: "Him who loved us and washed us from our sins in His own blood," and again in Revelation 7:14: "These are the ones who come out of the great tribulation, and washed their robes and made them white in the blood of the Lamb." Furthermore, we read in Galatians 3:27, "For as many of you as were baptized into Christ have put on Christ"; therefore, through baptism, we have put on Christ.

If at that point we say that we are not worthy of receiving communion, then we have devalued the precious Blood of our Lord. It is as if we are saying that the Blood of Christ is not enough to cleanse and purify us so that we would become worthy of being united with God. We might be tempted by such false thoughts; however, we need to be confident in the awesome power of our God, the Pantocrator, who can turn us sinners into saints, holy and set apart for His purpose.

More specifically, it is the Holy Spirit that sanctifies us through the Blood of our Lord, God, and Savior Jesus Christ. This is what is said in 1 Corinthians 6:11: "But you were washed, but you were sanctified, but you were justified in the name of the Lord Jesus and by the Spirit of our God." The Holy Spirit is the one who sanctifies us and makes us worthy of obtaining the unity with God through this sacrament. Our holiness pales in comparison to God; and in response to this, as we realize how unworthy we are of our own accord, we declare the holiness of the Trinity by saying, "One is the Holy Father, One is the Holy Son, One is the Holy Spirit. Amen." The very next prayer from the priest is an offering of peace to the congregation and, in response, to the priest as well. This prayer for peace is very important, particularly at this point, as it quells any fears or thoughts of unworthiness that one may have, encouraging us all to participate in communion.

"The Holy Body and the precious, True Blood of Jesus Christ, the Son of our God. Amen."

This is the beginning of the confession, declaring our belief that the Body and Blood of Christ are present with us on the altar. This is a declaration of faith in what our Lord Himself declared to us when He established for us this great sacrament. He said to His disciples, "Take, eat; this *is* My body," and again He said to them, "This *is* My blood of the new covenant." The disciples all ate and drank, though not yet fully understanding at that time; they believed that Christ gave them His Body and His Blood.

We also declare our belief that the holy Body and the true Blood of Jesus Christ are present with us at this moment. The entire congregation declares this by responding and saying, "Amen." Each of these three declarations are responded to in like manner. We all declare and confirm our faith and belief in this before we receive the Body and Blood of Christ.

"The Holy, Precious Body and the True Blood of Jesus Christ, the Son of our God. Amen."

Not only do we declare that this is the true Body and Blood of Christ, but we also declare that this is for us something very precious. In 1 Peter 1:19 we read that we were redeemed "with the precious blood of Christ, as of a lamb without blemish and without spot." We have come to realize and understand how precious this sacrament is to us. Saint Peter continues to describe this by his reference to Isaiah, which says,

> Behold, I lay in Zion
> A chief cornerstone, elect, precious,
> And he who believes on Him will by no
> means be put to shame. (1 Pt 2:6)

It is amazing to see how treasured our Lord and this sacrament is to the saints of the church. They entrusted everything to God to the point where they declared that He is their all in all. Saint Paul describes this when he says, "I have suffered the loss of all things, and count them as rubbish, that I may gain Christ" (Phil 3:8).

This is exactly what Christ describes to us when he uses the parable of the pearl of great price. He describes in Matthew, chapter 13, a merchant who found a very valuable pearl, and in order to buy it, he sold everything that he had. Those who really understand the value of this sacrament can understand why one would give up everything to attain unity with Christ. Once we are one with Christ, there is nothing more we need that God will not provide for us. How precious is this sacrament to us? As we respond with "amen," we should really ask ourselves if we honestly treasure this sacrament as much as we are declaring.

"The Body and the Blood of Emmanuel our God; this is true. Amen."

There is an amazing choice of words used here to describe the Body and Blood of Christ present on the altar with us. In Matthew 1:23, we read about the fulfillment of the prophesy made by Isaiah, who says, "Behold, the virgin shall be with child, and bear a Son, and they shall call His name Emmanuel, which is translated, 'God with us.'" There is no better way to describe this mystery than to describe our God by the name Emmanuel, essentially saying that God is with us.

When we say that this is the Body of Emmanuel or this is the Blood of Emmanuel our God, we are confirming two things. First, we are confirming our belief that this is without question the actual Body and Blood of Christ. Though to the senses it may look, feel, smell, and taste like bread and wine, we are affirming that this is no longer bread and wine but is actually the Body and the Blood of Our Lord God and Savior Jesus Christ. Second, and this is what makes our Christian faith so near and dear to our hearts, we are confirming that through this sacrament, God is present with us, not only spiritually present in our gathering but also physically present with us.

This is in fact a testimony to the humility and inherent greatness of God, that though we are part of the creation, God still loves us to such a great extent that there is no limit to how this love can be demonstrated. God, the all powerful, wondrous in glory, and Creator of all, is seeking to be present with us, the very people who have turned away and rejected God though sin. God is the one coming to us and looking for us to return again. When we receive communion, we hear these words, "the Body of Emmanuel our God, amen," or "the Blood of Emmanuel our God, amen." Our response to this should be a very clear and vocal "amen." In fact, at this third declaration, the congregation sings out emphatically, saying, "Amen, I believe."

"Amen. Amen. Amen. I believe, I believe, I believe and confess to the last breath that this is the life-giving Flesh that Your Only Begotten Son, our Lord, God, and Savior Jesus Christ..."

The confession declared at the end of liturgy captures the essence of our beliefs regarding this sacrament. It starts out with a declaration of our faith, particularly regarding our Lord Jesus Christ. Through this, we declare that Christ is the only begotten Son, who became man and took flesh, and that flesh is for us a source of life.

Saint John in his Gospel, as well as in his first epistle, points this out to us very clearly, indicating that Christ is the only begotten Son of the Father. In John 1:14 he says, "The Word became flesh and dwelt among us, and we beheld His glory, the glory as of the only begotten of the Father, full of grace and truth." Furthermore, he says later on, "No one has seen God at any time. The only begotten Son, who is in the bosom of the Father, He has declared *Him*" (Jn 1:18). By this we declare our belief that Christ is the only begotten Son of the Father, one of the Holy Trinity, God who became man for our salvation. This is what was declared in the famous verse from the Gospel of John:

> For God so loved the world that He gave
> His only begotten Son, that whoever

believes in Him should not perish but have everlasting life. (Jn 3:16)

This is reiterated again in his first epistle, which says, "the love of God was manifested toward us, that God has sent His only begotten Son into the world, that we might live through Him" (1 Jn 4:9). God's love for us has been revealed through the amazing work of salvation in the life of Christ.

The greatest sacrifice known to us is this, that Christ, who sits on His heavenly throne, forsook all glory to become human. All this He did out of the greatness of His love for us so that we can be saved. The death He suffered on the cross provides us with life. His body becomes a source of sustenance that leads to everlasting life. Here in this confession we declare that God's only begotten Son, His life, His body, His flesh is *life giving*. This Christ explains to us in the following passage:

> I am the living bread which came down from heaven. If anyone eats of this bread, he will live forever; and the bread that I shall give is My flesh, which I shall give for the life of the world. (Jn 6:51)

The main and essential purpose of the life of our Lord was to come down from heaven and return us back to our original condition. Describing this more eloquently, Saint Paul says, "And so it is written, 'The first man Adam became a living being.' The last Adam *became* a life-giving spirit" (1 Cor 15:45). The last Adam is none other than our Lord Jesus Christ.

When mankind fell from paradise, it was through the sin of Adam, and God knew the only way to restore us was to send to us His Son, to give life back to us. We have been restored through the life of Christ and are now a new creation. Through the resurrection, we now have new life because Christ destroyed the power death had over us. We are no longer bound by sin, but we have been given power over sin and death through this sacrament.

"Took from our lady, the lady of us all, the Holy Theotokos, Saint Mary."

The confession that is proclaimed at this time in liturgy is also a declaration of our faith and dogmatic beliefs. It presents us with the basic principles upon which our faith has been founded. While in the previous section we were declaring that Christ is the Son of God, come down from heaven to give life to His creation, in this portion, we are declaring that Christ is without question a human who was born of a woman.

This is very important for us to understand and believe, as this is crucial for our salvation. Since it was a man who caused the fall, it must be a man who restores us. Saint Athanasius explains, "By man death has gained its power over men; by the Word made Man death has been destroyed and life raised up anew" (*On the Incarnation,* chapter 2, section 10). Christ bore the penalty of death brought about by the sin in paradise; not only has He taken away from us this penalty, but He has also crushed the power of death through His resurrection. Redemption had to come through mankind, and this was accomplished by the incarnation—God became man.

Salvation had to come through God, who sent his only begotten Son to be incarnate and take flesh. God entered into the world and so was subject to the limitations of the world He created. In Galatians 4:4–5 this is explicitly stated, saying, "But when the fullness of the time had come, God sent forth His Son, born of a woman, born under the law, to redeem those who were under the law, that we might receive the adoption as sons." This is to say that our Lord, though He is God Almighty, was born and raised with all the restrictions of a human being. This means that like all others, He needed to eat, He felt tired, he felt thirsty, and was in fact human while still being divine.

Note that one of the terms used here is *Theotokos.* The literal translation of this word is "birth-giver of God" but is commonly translated as "Mother of God." This carries much significance and a very deep and important theological meaning. In fact, the dispute over this term was one of the main reasons for the Third Ecumenical Council, the Council of Ephesus. The main opponent of this term was Nestorius, who claimed that it would be wrong to call Saint Mary the *Theo*tokos, as he claimed that the divine nature of Christ was separate from the human nature. Therefore, he preferred the use of the term *Christo*tokos instead. This he believed was acceptable, as he claimed that she was capable of bearing the human nature of Christ but was not capable of bearing the divine nature.

Saint Cyril makes the following statement about this on page 55 in his book, *On the Unity of Christ*:

> He was born of a woman according to the flesh in a wondrous manner, for He is God by nature, as such invisible and incorporeal, and only in this way, in form like our own, could He be manifest to earthly creatures… This is what we mean when we say that He became flesh, and for the same reasons we affirm that the holy virgin is the Mother of God.

The use of the term *Theotokos* was upheld through this council with the explanation that the human nature and the divine nature of Christ are inseparable. Saint Cyril, the patriarch of Alexandria at that time, led this council and defended the faith against this heresy. In essence, by calling Saint Mary the Theotokos, we are confirming that Christ was united in His humanity and divinity from the moment of conception in her womb. The very next statement in this confession explains and confirms this unity.

"He made It One with His divinity without mingling, without confusion, and without alteration."

We continue to describe the fundamental beliefs of the church through this confession. It is important to understand this as an expression of the faith of the church. Here we see a summary of the teachings of Saint Cyril of Alexandria on who Christ is. These are the words he used to describe the unity of Christ:

> And indeed, the Only Begotten Word, even though He was God and born from God by nature, the "radiance of the glory, and the exact image of the being" of the one who begot Him (Heb 1:3), He it was who became man. He did not change Himself into flesh; He did not endure any mixture or blending, or anything else of this kind. But He submitted Himself to being emptied "for the sake of the honor that was set before Him He counted the shame as nothing" (Heb 12:2) and did not disdain the poverty of human nature. (*On the Unity of Christ*, 54)

Certainly we come to understand that the divinity of Christ was unified with His humanity without any mixing of the two. Saint Cyril describes this further by saying, "In the case of Christ [Godhood and manhood] came together in a mysterious and incomprehensible union, without confusion or change" (*On the Unity of Christ*, 77). The church utilizes this confession, with the Body and Blood of Christ present on the altar, to reiterate our faith on a weekly or even daily basis.

"He confessed the good confession before Pontius Pilate."

Now that we have established who Christ is through this confession, we go on to remember the confession Christ declared as He stood before Pontius Pilate. When our Lord was asked if He was a king, He responded, "My kingdom is not of this world" (Jn 18:36). We are reminded that we are not here looking for an earthly kingdom, but throughout the liturgy we are inspired to look up toward heaven. It is this heavenly kingdom that we are seeking and hoping to be part of through receiving the Body and Blood of Christ.

Christ declared and confessed to Pilate that He was a king. He said, "You say *rightly* that I am a king. For this cause I was born, and for this cause I have come into the world, that I should bear witness to the truth. Everyone who is of the truth hears My voice" (Jn 18:37). As Christ stands before him, Pilate asks, "What is truth?" Though he did not respond to this, we recall that Christ declared to us that He is the Way, the Truth, and the Life (Jn 14:6). What an amazing scene—there the answer to his question stood right before his eyes, but he could not see that Christ is the true king. He came down from His throne full of glory and humbly was born into this world in order to once again bring us back into His kingdom.

Saint Paul urges us to declare our faith to all just as Christ did before He was crucified for our sake. He says this in his epistle to Timothy:

> Fight the good fight of faith, lay hold on eternal life, to which you were also called and have confessed the good confession in the presence of many witnesses. I urge you in the sight of God who gives life to all things, and *before* Christ Jesus who witnessed the good confession before Pontius Pilate, that you keep *this* commandment without spot, blameless until our Lord Jesus Christ's appearing. (1 Tm 6:12–14)

We are all called to be witnesses to Christ, to share the good news with everyone who would accept it. Certainly, as Christians, we should not be hiding our faith but sharing and declaring it for all to see.

"He gave It up for us upon the Holy Wood of the Cross, of His own will, for us all."

Christ died on the cross for the sake of us sinners. He gave up His flesh for us willingly. This is not something that happened by chance, but God planned this for us to receive salvation. God has given us the gift of grace by choice, as we learn from Ephesians 1:11: "In Him also we have obtained an inheritance, being predestined according to the purpose of Him who works all things according to the counsel of His will." Saint James also reiterates this by saying, "Of His own will He brought us forth by the word of truth" (Jas 1:18).

We know that Christ was not forced to die for our sins, but He did so willingly. He expressed this to us plainly, saying, "Therefore My Father loves Me, because I lay down My life that I may take it again. No one takes it from Me, but I lay it down of Myself. I have power to lay it down, and I have power to take it again" (Jn 10:17–18). He is the good shepherd who has given his life for the sheep. This life, however, He has taken again through the resurrection. By this we have been cleansed from our sins and given eternal life.

"Truly I believe that His divinity parted not from His humanity for a single moment, nor a twinkling of an eye…"

We reiterate our belief that the divinity and the humanity of our Lord did not separate, not even for a single moment. Even in the death of our Lord on the cross, His divinity continued to be in union with His humanity, as the two are always united. The phrase used here, "for a single moment, nor a twinkling of an eye," has its roots in the words of Saint Paul as he spoke about our final victory. He explains that we will all be made incorruptible in order to inherit the kingdom of God. Specifically, he explains that this change will happen "in a moment, in the twinkling of an eye" (1 Cor 15:52). Christ, on the other hand, was always incorruptible and immortal, as His divinity was always united with His humanity, not separating even "for a single moment, nor a twinkling of an eye." In the Syrian Fraction, we understand this in a very important and unique way. It says, "His soul parted from His body, even though His divinity never parted, either from His soul or from His body." This is how the soul that is united to His divinity, went down to Hades to restore the saints to paradise, while His body that was laid in the tomb—also united to His divinity—never suffered corruption.

"Given for us for salvation, remission of sins, and eternal life to those who partake of Him."

Here we note three essential blessings for those of us who will go on to receive the Body and the Blood of Christ. We receive salvation, we receive forgiveness, and we receive eternal life. It is through this sacrament that we can attain the salvation offered to us through the death and resurrection of our Lord. Because Christ offered Himself as a pure and unblemished sacrifice, He was able to bear our sins. It is only through this true sacrifice that we are able to receive forgiveness. God has done this for us out of an abundance of love for us so that ultimately we may be united with Him in eternal life.

We proclaim that through this sacrifice offered on the altar, we have been given salvation. This salvation is a result of the forgiveness we receive because Christ took on our sins through His death on the cross. In the letter to the Ephesians we read, "In Him we have redemption through His blood, the forgiveness of sins, according to the riches of His grace" (Eph 1:7). We are reminded of what our Lord taught us as He instituted this sacrament for us, saying, "This is My blood of the new covenant, which is shed for many for the remission of sins" (Mt 26:28). Saint Paul reiterates this in Colossians 1:14: "In whom we have redemption through His blood, the forgiveness of sins." Without this sacrifice, we would be dead in our sins, but God has given us new life, as Saint Paul states, "And you *He made alive,* who were dead in trespasses and sins" (Eph 2:1).

The new life we have in Christ has been given to us through this sacrament. From the letter to the Hebrews, we can start to understand how the sacrifices offered by the temple priests before Christ were ineffective:

> And every priest stands ministering daily and offering repeatedly the same sacrifices, which can never take away sins. But this Man, after He had offered one sacrifice for sins forever, sat down at the right hand of God. (Heb 10:11–12)

This is the central purpose of our liturgical service; celebrating the new life that was given to us through the eternal sacrifice offered by Christ for our sins forever. Similarly stated in Hebrews 9:12, "Not with the blood of goats and calves, but with His own blood He entered the Most Holy Place once for all, having obtained eternal redemption." Not only have we received a new life, but this new life is eternal because we have an eternal redemption. There is no better reason for the celebration of the liturgy than what Christ has promised to those of us who receive communion:

> Whoever eats My flesh and drinks My blood
> has eternal life, and I will raise him up at the
> last day. (Jn 6:54)

We come together as one body in Christ, seeking to be liberated from the slavery of sin in order to gain eternal life with God.

I believe, I believe, I believe
that this is true.
Amen.

Liturgy of Saint Basil

with

Biblical References

Prayer of Reconciliation

Presbyter: O God, the Great,[1,2] the Eternal,[3] who formed man in incorruption, and death, which entered into the world through the envy of the devil,[4] You have destroyed by the life-giving manifestation of Your Only-Begotten Son, our Lord, God, and Savior Jesus Christ.[5] You have filled the earth with the Heavenly Peace by which the hosts of angels glorify You, saying, "Glory to God in the highest, peace on earth, and good will toward men."[6]

---

[1] Deuteronomy 10:17 – For the Lord your God *is* God of gods and Lord of lords, the great God, mighty and awesome, who shows no partiality nor takes a bribe.

[2] Psalm 95:3 – For the Lord is the great God, And the great King above all gods.

[3] 1 Timothy 1:17 – Now to the King eternal, immortal, invisible, to God who alone is wise, *be* honor and glory forever and ever. Amen.

[4] Wisdom 2:23-25 – For God created man incorruptible, and to the image of his own likeness he made him. But by the envy of the devil, death came into the world: And they follow him that are of his side. (Douay-Rheims 1899 American Edition DRA)

[5] Romans 5:17 – For if by the one man's offense death reigned through the one, much more those who receive abundance of grace and of the gift of righteousness will reign in life through the One, Jesus Christ.

[6] Luke 2:14 – "Glory to God in the highest, And on earth peace, goodwill toward men!"

Deacon: Pray for perfect peace, love, and the holy apostolic greetings.

Congregation: Lord have mercy.

Presbyter: According to your good will, O God, fill our hearts with your peace.[7] Cleanse us from all blemish, all guile, all hypocrisy, all malice, and the remembrance of evil, entailing death.[8] And make us all worthy, O our Master, to greet one another with a holy kiss.[9,10,11] That without falling into condemnation, we may partake of Your immortal and heavenly gift, in Christ Jesus, our Lord.

Deacon: Greet one another with a holy kiss.[9,10,11] Lord have mercy, Lord have mercy, Lord have mercy. Yea, Lord, who are Jesus Christ, the Son of God, hear us and

---

[7] Psalm 68:10 – Your congregation dwelt in it; You, O God, provided from Your goodness for the poor."

[8] 1 Peter 2:1-2 – Therefore, laying aside all malice, all deceit, hypocrisy, envy, and all evil speaking, as newborn babes, desire the pure milk of the word, that you may grow thereby.

[9] Romans 16:16 – Greet one another with a holy kiss.

[10] 2 Corinthians 13:12 – Greet one another with a holy kiss.

[11] 1 Peter 5:14 – Greet one another with a kiss of love.

have mercy upon us.[12,13,14] Offer (offer, offer) in order. Stand with trembling.[15,16] Look towards the East.[17,18] Let us attend.

Congregation: Through the intercessions of the Theotokos, Saint Mary, O Lord, grant us the forgiveness of our sins. We Worship You, O Christ, with Your Good Father and the Holy Spirit, for You (have come) and saved us.
A mercy of peace, a sacrifice of praise.[19]

---

[12] Matthew 20:30 – "Have mercy on us, O Lord, Son of David!"

[13] Mark 10:47 – "Jesus, Son of David, have mercy on me!"

[14] Luke 17:13 – "Jesus, Master, have mercy on us!"

[15] Psalm 33:8 – Let all the inhabitants of the world stand in awe of Him.

[16] Psalm119:161 – Princes persecute me without a cause, but my heart stands in awe of Your word.

[17] Ezekiel 43:2 – And behold, the glory of the God of Israel came from the way of the east.

[18] Matthew 24:27 – For as the lightning comes from the east and flashes to the west, so also will the coming of the Son of Man be.

[19] Hebrews 13:15 – Let us continually offer the sacrifice of praise to God, that is, the fruit of *our* lips, giving thanks to His name.

Anaphora

Presbyter: The Lord be with you all.[20,21]

Congregation: And with your spirit.[22,23]

Presbyter: Lift up your hearts.[24]

Congregation: We have them with the Lord.

Presbyter: Let us give thanks to the Lord.[25,26]

Congregation: It is meet and right.[27]

---

[20] Luke 1:28 – Rejoice, highly favored *one,* the Lord *is* with you.

[21] Galatians 6:18 – Brethren, the grace of our Lord Jesus Christ be with your spirit. Amen.

[22] 2 Timothy 4:22 – The Lord Jesus Christ be with your spirit. Grace be with you. Amen.

[23] Philemon 1:25 – The grace of our Lord Jesus Christ *be* with your spirit. Amen.

[24] Jeremiah 3:41 – Let us lift our hearts and hands to God in heaven.

[25] Psalm 118:1 – Oh, give thanks to the Lord, for He is good! For His mercy endures forever.

[26] Psalm 92:1 – It is good to give thanks to the Lord.

[27] Revelations 4:11 – You are worthy, O Lord to receive glory and honor and power.

Presbyter: Meet and right, meet and right, truly indeed, it is meet and right. O You, THE BEING, Master, Lord, God of Truth,[28] being before the ages, and reigning forever.[29,30] Who dwells in the highest and looks upon the lowly;[31] Who has created the heaven, the earth, the sea, and all that is therein. The Father of Our Lord, God, and Savior Jesus Christ. By whom You have created all things, visible and invisible.[32] Who sits upon the throne of His glory; and who is worshiped by all the holy powers.

Deacon: You who are seated, stand.

---

[28] Deuteronomy 32:4 – For all His ways are judgment, a _God of truth_ and without iniquity; _just and right is He_.

[29] Exodus 15:18 – The Lord shall _reign forever_ and ever.

[30] Revelations 11:15 – He shall reign forever and ever.

[31] Psalm 138:6 – Though the Lord is on high, yet He regards the lowly.

[32] Colossians 1:16 – For by Him all things were created that are in heaven and that are on earth, visible and invisible, whether thrones or dominions or principalities or powers. All things were created through Him and for Him.

Presbyter: Before whom stand the angels, the archangels,[33] the principalities, the authorities, the thrones, the dominions, and the powers.[34,35]

Deacon: Look towards the east.[36,37]

Presbyter: You are He, around whom stand the cherubim full of eyes,[38] and the seraphim with six wings,[39] praising continuously, without ceasing, saying:

Congregation: The Cherubim worship You, and the Seraphim glorify You, proclaiming and saying:

---

[33] Revelation 8:2 – And I saw the <u>seven angels who stand before God</u>.

[34] Ephesians 1:20-21 – Seated *Him* at His right hand in the heavenly *places,* far above all <u>principality and power and might and dominion</u>.

[35] Colossians 1:16 – For by Him all things were created that are in heaven and that are on earth, visible and invisible, <u>whether thrones or dominions or principalities or powers</u>.

[36] Ezekiel 43:2 – And behold, the <u>glory of the God of Israel came from the way of the east</u>.

[37] Matthew 24:27 – For as the <u>lightning comes from the east</u> and flashes to the west, so also will the <u>coming of the Son of Man be</u>.

[38] Ezekiel 10:12 – And their whole body, with their back, their hands, their wings, and the wheels that the four had, <u>*were* full of eyes all around</u>.

[39] Isaiah 6:2 – Above it stood <u>seraphim; each one had six wings</u>: with two he covered his face, with two he covered his feet, and with two he flew.

Holy, holy, holy, Lord of Hosts. Heaven and earth are full of Your Holy Glory.[40,41]

Presbyter: Holy, Holy, Holy indeed, O Lord our God. Who formed us,[42] created us, and placed us in the paradise of joy.

When we disobeyed Your commandment by the deception of the serpent, we fell from eternal life and were exiled from the paradise of joy.[43]

You have not abandoned us to the end, but have always visited us through Your Holy prophets.[44]

And in the last days You manifested Yourself to us,[45] who were sitting in darkness and the shadow of

---

[40] Isaiah 6:3 – <u>Holy, holy, holy *is* the Lord of hosts; The whole earth *is* full of His glory!</u>

[41] Revelations 4:8 – <u>Holy, holy, holy, Lord God Almighty, Who was and is and is to come!</u>

[42] Psalm 139:13 – <u>For You formed my inward parts.</u>

[43] Genesis 3:24 – <u>So He drove out the man; and He placed cherubim at the east of the garden of Eden,</u> and a flaming sword which turned every way, to guard the way to the tree of life.

[44] Matthew 23:27 – O Jerusalem, Jerusalem, the one who kills the prophets and stones those who are sent to her! <u>How often I wanted to gather your children together,</u> as a hen gathers her chicks under *her* wings, but you were not willing!

[45] Luke 7:16 – Then fear came upon all, and they glorified God, saying, "A great prophet has risen up among us"; and, "God has visited His people."

death.[46,47] Through Your Only-Begotten Son, our Lord, God, and Savior Jesus Christ, who, of the Holy Spirit and of the Holy Virgin Mary.[48,49]

Congregation: Amen.

Presbyter: Was incarnate and became man,[50] and taught us the ways of salvation.[51] He granted us the birth from on high through water and Spirit.[52] He made us unto

---

[46] Psalm 107:10 – Those who <u>sat in darkness and in the shadow of death</u>.

[47] Luke 1:78-79 – Through the tender mercy of our God, <u>with which the Dayspring from on high has visited us; To give light to those who sit in darkness and the shadow of death.</u>

[48] Matthew 1:18 – <u>She was found with child of the Holy Spirit</u>.

[49] Matthew 1:20 – <u>That which is conceived in her is of the Holy Spirit</u>.

[50] John 1:14 – <u>And the Word became flesh and dwelt among us.</u>

[51] Psalm 25:5 – Lead me in Your truth and <u>teach me</u>, for You _are_ the <u>God of my salvation</u>.

[52] John 3:5-6 – Most assuredly, I say to you, unless one is <u>born of water and the Spirit</u>, he cannot enter the kingdom of God.

Himself an assembled people,[53] and sanctified us by Your Holy Spirit.[54]

He loved His own who were in the world,[55] and as a ransom on our behalf, gave Himself up unto death,[56] which reigned over us, whereby we were bound and sold on account of our sins.[57,58,59] He descended into Hades through the cross.[60,61]

---

[53] Hebrews 12:23 – <u>The general assembly and church of the firstborn</u> *who are* registered in heaven.

[54] Colossians 6:11 – You were <u>washed</u>, but you were <u>sanctified</u>, but you were justified in the name of the Lord Jesus and <u>by the Spirit of our God</u>.

[55] John 13:1 – Having <u>loved His own who were in the world</u>, He loved them to the end.

[56] 1 Timothy 2:6 – <u>Who gave Himself a ransom for all</u>.

[57] Acts 8:32 – For I see that you are poisoned by bitterness and <u>bound by iniquity</u>.

[58] Psalm 107:10 – Those who sat in darkness and in the shadow of death, <u>bound in affliction and irons— because they rebelled against the words of God</u>, and despised the counsel of the Most High.

[59] Romans 6:23 – For the <u>wages of sin</u> *is* <u>death</u>, but the <u>gift of God</u> *is* <u>eternal life</u> in Christ Jesus our Lord.

[60] Ephesians 4:9-10 – Now this, 'He ascended'—what does it mean but that He also first <u>descended into the lower parts of the earth</u>?

[61] Acts 2:31 – Concerning the resurrection of the Christ, that <u>His soul was not left in Hades</u>, nor did His flesh see corruption.

Congregation: Amen, I believe.

Presbyter: He rose from the dead on the third day.[62,63] He ascended into the Heavens and sat at Your Right Hand, O Father.[64,65] He has appointed a day for recompense, on which He will appear to judge the world in righteousness,[66] and give each one according to his deeds.[67]

Congregation: According to Your mercy, O Lord, and not according to our sins.

---

[62] Acts 10:40 – Him God raised up on the third day, and showed Him openly.

[63] 1 Corinthians 15:4 – He rose again the third day.

[64] Mark 16:19 – He was received up into heaven, and sat down at the right hand of God.

[65] Luke 22:69 – Hereafter the Son of Man will sit on the right hand of the power of God.

[66] Acts 17:31 – He has appointed a day on which He will judge the world in righteousness.

[67] Romans 2:5-6 – The righteous judgment of God, who will render to each one according to his deeds.

The Institution Narrative

Presbyter: He instituted[68] for us this great Mystery of Godliness.[69] For being determined[70] to give Himself up to death for the life of the world.[71,72]

Congregation: We Believe.

Presbyter: He took bread[68] into His Holy Hands, which are without spot, or blemish, blessed, and Life Giving.[73]

Congregation: We believe that this is true. Amen.

---

[68] 1 Corinthians 11:23 – <u>For I received from the Lord</u> that which I also delivered to you: that <u>the Lord Jesus</u> on the same night in which He was betrayed <u>took bread</u>.

[69] Timothy 3:16 – And without controversy great is the <u>mystery of godliness</u>: God was manifested in the flesh, justified in the Spirit, Seen by angels, Preached among the Gentiles, Believed on in the world, Received up in glory.

[70] Acts 2:23 – Him, being delivered by the <u>determined purpose</u> and foreknowledge of God, you have taken by lawless hands, have crucified, and <u>put to death</u>.

[71] John 15:13 – Greater love has no one than this, than to lay down one's life for his friends.

[72] John 6:33 – For the bread of God is He who comes down from heaven and <u>gives life to the world</u>.

[73] 1 Peter 1:19 – The precious blood of Christ, as of a lamb <u>without blemish and without spot</u>.

Presbyter: He looked up[74] toward Heaven to You, O God, who are His Father and Master of everyone.
And when He had given thanks.[75,76]

Congregation: Amen.

Presbyter: He blessed it.[77,78]

Congregation: Amen.

Presbyter: He sanctified it.

Congregation: Amen. We believe, we confess, and we glorify.

Presbyter: He broke it, and gave it to His own saintly disciples and Holy apostles, saying, 'Take, eat of It, all of

---

[74] Mark 6:41 – When He had taken the five loaves and the two fish, He looked up to heaven, blessed and broke the loaves, and gave them to His disciples to set before them.
[75] Luke 22:19 – And He took bread, gave thanks and broke *it*…
[76] 1 Corinthians 11:24 – and when He had given thanks, He broke *it*…
[77] Matthew 26:26 – And as they were eating, Jesus took bread, blessed and broke *it*…
[78] Mark 14:22 – And as they were eating, Jesus took bread, blessed and broke *it*…

you, for this is My Body, which is broken for you and for many, to be given for the remission of sins. This do in remembrance of Me.' [79,80,81,82]

Congregation: This is true. Amen.

---

[79] Matthew 26:26 – And as they were eating, Jesus took bread, blessed and broke *it,* and gave *it* to the disciples and said, "Take, eat; this is My body."

[80] Mark 14:22 – And as they were eating, Jesus took bread, blessed and broke *it,* and gave *it* to them and said, "Take, eat; this is My body."

[81] Luke 22:19 – And He took bread, gave thanks and broke *it,* and gave *it* to them, saying, "This is My body which is given for you; do this in remembrance of Me."

[82] 1 Corinthians 11:23-24 – For I received from the Lord that which I also delivered to you: that the Lord Jesus on the *same* night in which He was betrayed took bread; and when He had given thanks, He broke *it* and said, "Take, eat; this is My body which is broken for you; do this in remembrance of Me."

Presbyter: Likewise also, the cup, after supper,[83,84] He mixed it with wine and water. And when He had given thanks.[85,86]

Congregation: Amen.

Presbyter: He blessed it.

Congregation: Amen.

Presbyter: He sanctified it.

Congregation: Amen. Again we believe, we confess, and we glorify.

Presbyter: He tasted, and gave It also to His own saintly disciples and Holy apostles, saying, 'Take drink of It all of you, for this is My Blood of the New Covenant, which

---

[83] Luke 22:20 – Likewise He also *took* the cup after supper.

[84] 1 Corinthians 11:25 – In the same manner *He* also *took* the cup after supper…

[85] Matthew 26:27 – Then He took the cup, and gave thanks…

[86] Mark 14:23 – Then He took the cup, and when He had given thanks…

is shed for you and for many, to be given for the remission of sins. in remembrance of Me.'[87,88,89,90]

Congregation: This is also true. Amen.

Presbyter: "For every time you eat of this bread and drink of this cup, you proclaim My Death, confess My Resurrection, and remember Me till I come." [91]

Congregation: Amen, Amen, Amen. Your death, O Lord, we proclaim. Your holy resurrection, and ascension into

---

[87] Matthew 26:27-28 – Then He took the cup, and gave thanks, and gave *it* to them, saying, "Drink from it, all of you. For this is My blood of the new covenant, which is shed for many for the remission of sins.

[88] Mark 14:23-24 – Then He took the cup, and when He had given thanks He gave *it* to them, and they all drank from it. And He said to them, "This is My blood of the new covenant, which is shed for many.

[89] Luke 22:20 – Likewise He also *took* the cup after supper, saying, "This cup *is* the new covenant in My blood, which is shed for you.

[90] 1 Corinthians 11:25 – In the same manner *He* also *took* the cup after supper, saying, "This cup is the new covenant in My blood. This do, as often as you drink *it*, in remembrance of Me."

[91] 1 Corinthians 11:26 – For as often as you eat this bread and drink this cup, you proclaim the Lord's death till He comes.

the heavens, we confess. We praise You, we bless You, we thank You, O Lord, and we entreat You, O our God.

Presbyter: Therefore, as we also commemorate His Holy Passion, His Resurrection from the dead, His Ascension into the heavens, His sitting at Your right[92,93,94] hand, O Father, and His Second Coming from the heavens, awesome and full of glory.[95]

We offer unto You Your gifts from what is Yours, for everything, concerning everything, and in everything.[96]

Deacon: Worship God in fear and trembling.

---

[92] Luke 22:69 – Hereafter the <u>Son of Man will sit on the right hand of the power of God</u>.

[93] Mark 16:19 – So then, after the Lord had spoken to them, He was received up into heaven, <u>and sat down at the right hand of God</u>.

[94] Colossians 3:1 – If then you were raised with Christ, seek those things which are above, <u>where Christ is, sitting at the right hand of God</u>.

[95] 1 Thessalonians 4:16-17 – For the <u>Lord Himself will descend from heaven with a shout, with the voice of an archangel, and with the trumpet of God</u>. And the dead in Christ will rise first. Then we who are alive *and* remain shall be caught up together with them in the clouds to meet the Lord in the air.

[96] 1 Thessalonians 5:16-18 – Rejoice always, pray without ceasing, <u>in everything give thanks</u>; for this is the will of God in Christ Jesus for you.

Congregation: We praise You, we bless You, we serve You, we worship You.

Deacon: Let us attend. Amen.

Presbyter: And this bread He makes into His Holy Body.

Congregation: I believe. Amen.

Presbyter: And this cup also, the Precious Blood of His New Covenant.

Congregation: Again, I believe. Amen.

Presbyter: Our Lord, God and Savior Jesus Christ, given for the remission of sins and eternal life to those who partake of Him.[97,98]

Congregation: Lord have mercy, Lord have mercy, Lord have mercy.

---

[97] John 6:51 – I am the living bread which came down from heaven. If anyone eats of this bread, he will live forever; and the bread that I shall give is My flesh, which I shall give for the life of the world.

[98] John 6:58 – This is the bread which came down from heaven—not as your fathers ate the manna, and are dead. He who eats this bread will live forever.

The Seven Litanies

Presbyter: Make us all worthy,[99] O our Master, to partake of Your Holies,[100] unto the purification of souls, bodies, and our spirits, that we may become one body and one spirit,[101,102,103,104] and may have a share and inheritance with all the saints who have pleased You since the beginning.[100, 105]

Remember, O Lord, the peace of Your One, Only, Holy, catholic, and Apostolic Church.

---

[99] 1 Corinthians 11:27 – Therefore whoever eats this bread or drinks _this_ cup of the Lord in an unworthy manner will be guilty of the body and blood of the Lord.

[100] Colossians 1:12 – Giving thanks to the Father who has <u>qualified us to be partakers of the inheritance of the saints</u> in the light.

[101] Romans 12:5 – So we, _being_ many, are <u>one body in Christ</u>, and individually members of one another.

[102] 1 Corinthians 10:17 – For we, _though_ many, are one bread _and_ <u>one body</u>; for we all partake of that one bread.

[103] 1 Corinthians 12:13 – For by <u>one Spirit we were all baptized into one body</u>.

[104] Ephesians 4:4 – _There is_ <u>one body and one Spirit</u>, just as you were called in one hope of your calling.

[105] Hebrews 9:15 – That those who are called may receive the <u>promise of the eternal inheritance</u>.

Deacon: Pray for the peace of the one, holy, catholic, and apostolic Orthodox Church of God.

Congregation: Lord have mercy.

Presbyter: This, which You have acquired to Yourself with the Precious Blood of Your Christ,[106,107] keep her in peace, with all the Orthodox Bishops who are in her. Foremost remember, O Lord, our blessed and honored father, the archbishop, our patriarch Pope Abba *(n.)*, and his partner in the (apostolic) liturgy, our father the Bishop Abba *(n.)*.

Deacon: Pray for our high priest, Pope Abba *(n.)*. Pope and patriarch and archbishop of the great city of Alexandria; And his partner in the apostolic liturgy, our father the Bishop, Abba *(n.)*, and for our Orthodox Bishops.

---

[106] 1 Peter 1:18-19 — You were not redeemed with corruptible things, *like* silver or gold, from your aimless conduct *received* by tradition from your fathers, but with the precious blood of Christ, as of a lamb without blemish and without spot.

[107] Acts 20:28 — Therefore take heed to yourselves and to all the flock, among which the Holy Spirit has made you overseers, to shepherd the church of God which He purchased with His own blood.

Congregation: Lord have mercy.

Presbyter: And those who rightly handle the Word of Truth[108] with him, grant them unto Your Holy Church to shepherd Your flock in peace.[109,110] Remember, O Lord, the Orthodox hegomens, Priests, and deacons.

Deacons: Pray for the hegomens, Priests, deacons, subdeacons, and the seven orders of the Church of God.

Congregation: Lord have mercy.

Presbyter: And all the servants, all who are in virginity, and the purity of all Your faithful people. Remember, O Lord, to have mercy upon us all.[111]

---

[108] 2 Timothy 2:15 – Be diligent to present yourself approved to God, a worker who does not need to be ashamed, rightly dividing the word of truth.

[109] Acts 20:28 – Therefore take heed to yourselves and to all the flock, among which the Holy Spirit has made you overseers, to shepherd the church of God which He purchased with His own blood.

[110] 1 Peter 5:2 – Shepherd the flock of God which is among you, serving as overseers, not by compulsion but willingly.

[111] 1 Peter 2:10 – Who once _were_ not a people but _are_ now the people of God, who had not obtained mercy but now have obtained mercy.

Congregation: Have mercy upon us, O God, the Father, the Pantocrator.

Presbyter: Remember, O Lord, the salvation of this, Your Holy place, and every place, and every monastery of our Orthodox Fathers.[112]

Deacon: Pray for the salvation of this world and of this city of ours, and of all cities, countries, islands, and monasteries.

Congregation: Lord have mercy.

Presbyter: And those who dwell therein in God's faith.[113] Graciously accord, O Lord, to bless the air of heaven, the fruits of the earth, the waters of the river, the seeds, the herbs, and the plants of the field this year.

Deacon: Pray for the air of heaven, the fruits of the earth, the rising of the waters of the rivers, the seeds, the herbs, and the plants of the field, that Christ our God may bless them, have compassion on His creation which His Hands have made, and forgive us our sins.

---

[112] Psalm 4:8 – I will both lie down in peace, and sleep; for You alone, O Lord, make me dwell in safety.
[113] Ephesians 3:17 – That Christ may dwell in your hearts through faith.

Congregation: Lord have mercy, Lord have mercy, Lord have mercy.

Presbyter: Raise them to their measure according to Your Grace.[114] Give joy to the face of the earth.[115] May its furrows be abundantly watered and its fruits be plentiful. [116] Prepare it for sowing and harvesting. Manage our lives as deemed fit. Bless the crown of the year with Your goodness,[117] for the sake of the poor of Your people, the widow, the orphan, the traveler, the stranger, and for the sake of us all who entreat You and seek Your Holy Name. For the eyes of everyone wait upon You, for You give them their food in due season.[118,119]

---

[114] Ephesians 4:7 – <u>But to each one of us grace was given according to the measure of Christ's gift</u>.

[115] Psalms 104:30 – You send forth Your Spirit, they are created; <u>and You renew the face of the earth.</u>

[116] Psalms 65:10 – You <u>water its ridges abundantly, You settle its furrows</u>; You make it soft with showers, <u>You bless its growth</u>.

[117] Psalm 65:11 – <u>You crown the year with Your goodness,</u> and Your paths drip with abundance.

[118] Psalms 145:14-16 – The Lord upholds all who fall, and raises up all who are bowed down. <u>The eyes of all look expectantly to You, and You give them their food in due season.</u>

[119] Psalms 104:27 – <u>These all wait for You, that You may give them their food in due season.</u>

Deal with us according to Your goodness, O You who give food to all flesh.[120] Fill our hearts with joy and gladness,[121] that we too, having sufficiency in everything always, may abound in every good deed.[122]

Congregation: Lord have mercy.

Presbyter: Remember, O Lord, those who brought to You these gifts, those on whose behalf they have been brought, and those by whom they have been brought. Give them all the Heavenly reward.

Deacon: Pray for these Holy and precious gifts, our sacrifices, and those who bring them.

Congregation: Lord have mercy.

---

[120] Psalms 136:25 – Who gives food to all flesh, for His mercy endures forever.

[121] Acts 14:17 – Nevertheless He did not leave Himself without witness, in that He did good, gave us rain from heaven and fruitful seasons, filling our hearts with food and gladness.

[122] 2 Corinthians 9:8 – And God *is* able to make all grace abound toward you, that you, always having all sufficiency in all things, may have an abundance for every good work.

The Commemoration

Presbyter: As this, O Lord, is the command of Your Only Begotten Son, that we share in the commemoration of Your saints. [123],[124] Graciously accord, O Lord, to remember all the saints who have pleased You since the beginning: our Holy fathers the patriarchs, the prophets, the apostles, the preachers, the evangelists, the martyrs, and the confessors and all the spirits of the righteous perfected in the faith.[125,126]

Most of all, the pure, full-of-Glory, Ever-virgin, Holy Theotokos, Saint Mary, who truly gave birth to God the Logos.

---

[123] Hebrews 13:7 – Remember those who rule over you, who have spoken the word of God to you, whose faith follow, considering the outcome of *their* conduct.

[124] Matthew 26:13 and Mark 14:9 – Assuredly, I say to you, wherever this gospel is preached in the whole world, what this woman has done will also be told as a memorial to her.

[125] Hebrews 12:22-24 – But you have come to Mount Zion and to the city of the living God, the heavenly Jerusalem, to an innumerable company of angels, to the general assembly and church of the firstborn who are registered in heaven, to God the Judge of all, <u>to the spirits of just men made perfect,</u> to Jesus the Mediator of the new covenant.

[126] James 2:22 – Do you see that faith was working together with his works, and <u>by works faith was made perfect?</u>

And Saint John the forerunner, Baptist, and martyr; Saint Stephen the archdeacon and protomartyr; the beholder-of-God the evangelist Mark, the holy apostle and martyr.

The patriarch Saint Severus; our teacher Dioscorus; Saint Athanasius the Apostolic; Saint Peter, the Holy martyr and high priest.

Saint John Chrysostom; Saint Theodosius; Saint Theophilus; Saint Demetrius; Saint Cyril; Saint Basil; Saint Gregory the theologian; Saint Gregory the wonder worker; Saint Gregory the Armenian.

The three hundred and eighteen assembled at Nicea; the one hundred and fifty at Constantinople; and the two hundred at Ephesus.

Our righteous father, the great Abba Anthony; the righteous Abba Paul; the three saints Abba Macarii and all their children, the cross-bearers; our father Abba John the hegomen; our righteous father Abba Pishoy, the perfect man, the beloved of our good Savior.

Our father Abba Paul of Tammoh and Ezekiel his disciple; my lords, the Roman fathers Saints Maximus and Dometius; the forty nine martyrs; the elders of Shiheet; the strong Saint Abba Moses; John Kame the priest; our father Abba Daniel the hegomen; our father

Abba Isidore the priest; our father Abba Pachom of the Koinonia, and Theodore his disciple; our father Abba Shenoute the archimandrite, and Abba Wesa, his disciple.

And all the choir of Your saints, through whose prayers and supplications, have mercy on us all, and save us, for the sake of Your Holy Name, which is called upon us.[127,128]

Deacon: Let those who read recite the names of our Holy Fathers, the patriarchs who have fallen asleep: O Lord, repose their souls and forgive us our sins.

Congregation: May their holy blessings be with us. Amen. Glory to You, O Lord. Lord have mercy. Lord have mercy. Lord, bless us. Lord, repose them. Amen.

---

[127] Psalm 115:1 – Not unto us, O Lord, not unto us, but to Your name give glory, because of Your mercy, because of Your truth.

[128] 2 Chronicles 7:14-15 – If My people who are called by My name will humble themselves, and pray and seek My face, and turn from their wicked ways, then I will hear from heaven, and will forgive their sin and heal their land. Now My eyes will be open and My ears attentive to prayer made in this place.

Introduction to the Fraction

Presbyter: Those, O Lord, whose souls You have taken, repose them in the paradise of joy,[129,130] in the region of the living for ever, in the Heavenly Jerusalem[131] in that place. And we too, who are sojourners in this

---

[129] Genesis 2:8-9 – The Lord God planted a <u>garden</u> eastward <u>in Eden</u>, and there He put the man whom He had formed. And out of the ground the Lord God made every tree grow that is pleasant to the sight and good for food. <u>The tree of life</u> *was* also in the midst of the garden, and the tree of the knowledge of good and evil.

[130] Revelation 2:7 – To him who overcomes I will give to eat from the <u>tree of life</u>, which is in the midst of the <u>Paradise of God</u>.

[131] Hebrews 12:22 – But you have come to Mount Zion and to <u>the city of the living God, the heavenly Jerusalem</u>, to an innumerable company of angels.

place,[132,133,134] keep us in Your faith, and grant us Your peace unto the end.[135,136]

Congregation: As it was, and shall be, it is from generation to generation,[137] and all the ages of the ages. Amen.

---

[132] 1 Chronicles 29:15 – For <u>we are aliens and pilgrims</u> before You, as were all our fathers; our days on earth are as a shadow.

[133] Hebrews 11:13-14 – <u>died in faith… and confessed that they were strangers and pilgrims on the earth</u>. For those who say such things declare plainly that they seek a homeland.

[134] 1 Peter 2:11 – Beloved, I beg you <u>as sojourners and pilgrims</u>, abstain from fleshly lusts which war against the soul.

[135] Romans 8:6 – For to be carnally minded *is* death, but <u>to be spiritually minded</u> *is* <u>life and peace</u>.

[136] Philippians 4:7 – The <u>peace of God, which surpasses all understanding</u> will guard your hearts and minds through Christ Jesus.

[137] Ephesians 3:21 – to Him *be* glory in the church by Christ Jesus <u>to all generations, forever and ever. Amen</u>.

Presbyter: Lead us throughout the way into Your kingdom,[138,139,140] that as in this, so also in all things, Your Great and Holy Name may be glorified,[141,142,143,144] blessed and exalted in everything, honored and blessed with Jesus Christ, Your Beloved Son, and the Holy Spirit.

Peace be with all.

Congregation: And with your spirit.

---

[138] 2 Corinthians 2:14 – Now thanks be to <u>God who always leads us in triumph in Christ</u>.

[139] Psalms 27:11 – <u>Teach me Your way, O Lord, and lead me in a smooth path</u>, because of my enemies.

[140] Psalms 139:24 – And see if *there is any* wicked way in me, <u>and lead me in the way everlasting</u>.

[141] Psalms 23:3 – <u>He leads me in the paths of righteousness for His name's sake.</u>

[142] Psalm 31:3 –For You *are* my rock and my fortress; therefore, <u>for Your name's sake, lead me and guide me</u>.

[143] Isaiah 63:14 – You lead Your people, <u>to make Yourself a glorious name</u>.

[144] 2 Thessalonians 1:11-12 – Therefore we also pray always for you that our God would count you worthy of *this* calling, and fulfill all the good pleasure of *His* goodness and the work of faith with power, that <u>the name of our Lord Jesus Christ may be glorified in you</u>, and you in Him, according to the grace of our God and the Lord Jesus Christ.

Presbyter: Again, let us give thanks to God the Pantocrator,[145,146,147] the Father of our Lord, God, and Savior Jesus Christ, for He also has made us worthy[148,149]

---

145 Psalms 30:4 – Sing praise to the Lord, you saints of His, and give thanks at the remembrance of His holy name.

146 Psalms 97:12 – Rejoice in the Lord, you righteous, and give thanks at the remembrance of His holy name.

147 1 Chronicles 16:35 – To give thanks to Your holy name, to triumph in Your praise.

148 2 Thessalonians 1:11 – Therefore we also pray always for you that our God would count you worthy of _this_ calling, and fulfill all the good pleasure of _His_ goodness and the work of faith with power.

149 Colossians 1:12 – Giving thanks to the Father who has qualified us to be partakers of the inheritance of the saints in the light.

now to stand in this Holy Place,[150,151,152] to lift up our hands[153,154,155] and to serve His Holy Name.[156]

---

150 Exodus 3:5 – Do not draw near this place. Take your sandals off your feet, for <u>the place where you stand *is* holy ground</u>.

151 Psalms 24:3 – Who may ascend into the hill of the Lord? Or <u>who may stand in His holy place?</u>

152 Luke 21:36 – Watch therefore, and pray always that you may be <u>counted worthy</u> to escape all these things that will come to pass, and <u>to stand before the Son of Man</u>.

153 Psalms 63:4 – Thus I will bless You while I live; <u>I will lift up my hands in Your name</u>.

154 Psalm 134:2 – <u>Lift up your hands *in* the sanctuary</u>, and bless the Lord.

155 Psalm 141:2 – Let my prayer be set before You *as* incense, <u>the lifting up of my hands *as* the evening sacrifice</u>.

156 1 Timothy 1:12 – And <u>I thank Christ Jesus our Lord</u> who has enabled me, because <u>He counted me faithful,</u> <u>putting *me* into the ministry</u>.

Let us also ask Him to make us worthy of the communion and partaking of His Divine and Immortal Mysteries.[157]

Congregation: Amen.

Presbyter: The Holy Body

Congregation: We worship Your Holy Body

Presbyter: And the Precious Blood.

Congregation: And Your Precious Blood.

Presbyter: Of His Christ, the Pantocrator, the Lord Our God.

Deacon: Amen. Amen. Let us pray.

Congregation: Lord have mercy.

Presbyter: Peace be with all.

Congregation: And with your spirit.
(Here a fraction is chosen according to the liturgical season.)

---

[157] Corinthians 11:27 – Therefore whoever eats this bread or drinks *this* cup of the Lord in an unworthy manner will be guilty of the body and blood of the Lord.

Presbyter: To pray to You, O God, the holy Father who is in the heavens, and say:

Congregation: Our Father who art in heaven, hallowed be Thy name. Thy kingdom come, Thy will be done, on earth as it is in heaven. Give us this day our daily bread; and forgive us our trespasses, as we forgive those who trespass against us; and lead us not into temptation, but deliver us from the evil one. In Christ Jesus our Lord, for Thine is the kingdom, the power, and the glory forever. Amen.[158,159]

Deacon: Bow your heads to the Lord.

Congregation: Before You, O Lord.

Deacon: Let us attend in the fear of God. Amen.

---

[158] Matthew 6:9-13 – Our Father in heaven, hallowed be Your name. Your kingdom come. Your will be done, on earth as *it is* in heaven. Give us this day our daily bread. and forgive us our debts, as we forgive our debtors. And do not lead us into temptation, but deliver us from the evil one. For Yours is the kingdom and the power and the glory forever. Amen.

[159] Luke 11:2-4 – Our Father in heaven, hallowed be Your name. Your kingdom come. Your will be done on earth as *it is* in heaven. Give us day by day our daily bread. And forgive us our sins, for we also forgive everyone who is indebted to us. And do not lead us into temptation, but deliver us from the evil one.

Presbyter: Peace be with all.

Congregation: And with your spirit.

Presbyter: Remember, O Lord, our assemblies; bless them.

Deacon: Saved. Amen. And with your spirit. In the fear of God, let us attend.

Congregation: Amen. Lord have mercy. Lord have mercy. Lord have mercy.

The Confession

Presbyter: The Holies for the holy.[160,161] Blessed be the Lord Jesus Christ, the Son of God; the sanctification is by the Holy Spirit.[162] Amen.

Congregation: One is the Holy Father, one is the Holy Son, one is the Holy Spirit. Amen.

Presbyter: Peace be with all.

Congregation: And with your spirit.

---

[160] 1 Peter 1:16 – Be holy, for I am holy.

[161] John 17:16-19 – They are not of the world, just as I am not of the world. Sanctify them by Your truth. Your word is truth. As You sent Me into the world, I also have sent them into the world. And for their sakes I sanctify Myself, that they also may be sanctified by the truth.

[162] 1 Corinthians 6:11 – But you were washed, but you were sanctified, but you were justified in the name of the Lord Jesus and by the Spirit of our God.

Presbyter: The Holy Body[163,164,165,166] and the precious,[167,168] true Blood[169,170,171,172] of Jesus Christ, the Son of our God.[173, 174,175] Amen.

---

163 Matthew 26:26 – And as they were eating, Jesus took bread, blessed and broke _it,_ and gave _it_ to the disciples and said, "Take, eat; this is My body."

164 Mark 14:22 – And as they were eating, Jesus took bread, blessed and broke _it,_ and gave _it_ to them and said, "Take, eat; this is My body."

165 Luke 22:19 – And He took bread, gave thanks and broke _it,_ and gave _it_ to them, saying, "This is My body."

166 1 Corinthians 11:24 – And when He had given thanks, He broke _it_ and said, "Take, eat; this is My body."

167 Isaiah 28:16 – Behold, I lay in Zion a stone for a foundation, a tried stone, a precious cornerstone, a sure foundation.

168 1 Peter 1:19 – With the precious blood of Christ, as of a lamb without blemish and without spot.

169 Matthew 26:28 – For this is My blood of the new covenant.

170 Mark 14:24 – This is My blood of the new covenant.

171 Luke 22:20 –This cup _is_ the new covenant in My blood.

172 1 Corinthians 11:25 –This cup is the new covenant in My blood.

173 Mark 1:1 – The beginning of the gospel of Jesus Christ, the Son of God.

174 Luke 1:35 – Therefore, also, that Holy One who is to be born will be called the Son of God.

175 1 John 5:12 - He who has the Son has life; he who does not have the Son of God does not have life.

Congregation: Amen.

Presbyter: The Holy, precious[167,168] Body[163,164,165,168] and the true Blood[169,170,171,172] of Jesus Christ, the Son of our God.[173,174,175] Amen.
Congregation: Amen.

Presbyter: The Body and the Blood of Emmanuel our God;[176,177] this is true. Amen.

Congregation: Amen. I believe.

Presbyter: Amen. Amen. Amen. I believe, I believe, I believe and confess to the last breath that this is the life-giving Flesh[178,179] that Your only-begotten Son, our

---

[176] Isaiah 7:14 – Therefore the Lord Himself will give you a sign: Behold, the virgin shall conceive and bear a Son, and shall call <u>His name Emmanuel</u>.
[177] Matthew 1:23 – Behold, the virgin shall be with child, and bear a Son, and they shall <u>call His name Immanuel,"</u> <u>which is translated, "God with us."</u>
[178] John 6:51 – I am the <u>living bread</u> which came down from heaven. <u>If anyone eats of this bread, he will live</u> <u>forever;</u> and <u>the bread that I shall give is My flesh, which I</u> <u>shall give for the life of the world.</u>
[179] 1 Corinthians 15:45 – 'The first man Adam became a living being.' The last Adam *became* a <u>life-giving spirit</u>.

Lord, God, and Savior Jesus Christ,[180,181,182,183] took from our lady, the lady of us all, the Holy Theotokos, Saint Mary.[184] He made It one with His divinity without mingling, without confusion, and without alteration. He confessed the good confession before Pontius Pilate.[185]

[180] John 1:14 – The Word <u>became flesh</u> and dwelt among us, and we beheld His glory, the glory as of <u>the only begotten of the Father</u>, full of grace and truth.

[181] John 1:18 – No one has seen God at any time. The <u>only begotten Son</u>, who is in the bosom of the Father, He has declared *Him*.

[182] John 3:16 – For God so loved the world that He gave His <u>only begotten Son</u>, that whoever believes in Him should not perish but have everlasting life.

[183] 1 John 4:9 - The love of God was manifested toward us, that God has sent His <u>only begotten Son</u> into the world, that we might live through Him.

[184] Galatians 4:4-5 – But when the fullness of the time had come, <u>God sent forth His Son, born of a woman</u>, born under the law, to redeem those who were under the law, that we might receive the adoption as sons.

[185] 1 Timothy 6:13-14 – I urge you in the sight of God who gives life to all things, and *before* <u>Christ Jesus who witnessed the good confession before Pontius Pilate</u>, that you keep *this* commandment without spot, blameless until our Lord Jesus Christ's appearing.

He gave It up for us upon the Holy Wood of the Cross, of His own will,[186,187,188] for us all.

Truly I believe that His divinity parted not from His humanity for a single moment, nor a twinkling of an

---

[186] Ephesians 1:11 – In Him also we have obtained an inheritance, being predestined according to the purpose of Him who works all things <u>according to the counsel of His will</u>.

[187] James 1:18 – <u>Of His own will</u> He brought us forth by the word of truth.

[188] John 10:17-18 – "Therefore My Father loves Me, because I lay down My life that I may take it again. <u>No one takes it from Me, but I lay it down of Myself.</u> I have power to lay it down, and I have power to take it again."

eye;[189] given for us for salvation, remission of sins, and eternal life to those who partake of Him.[190,191,192,193,194]

I believe, I believe, I believe that this is true. Amen.

---

[189] 1 Corinthians 15:51-52 – Behold, I tell you a mystery: We shall not all sleep, but we shall all be changed— in a moment, in the twinkling of an eye, at the last trumpet. For the trumpet will sound, and the dead will be raised incorruptible, and we shall be changed.

[190] Ephesians 1:7 – In Him we have redemption through His blood, the forgiveness of sins, according to the riches of His grace.

[191] Matthew 26:28 – This is My blood of the new covenant, which is shed for many for the remission of sins.

[192] Colossians 1:14 – In whom we have redemption through His blood, the forgiveness of sins.

[193] Hebrews 9:12, " Not with the blood of goats and calves, but with His own blood He entered the Most Holy Place once for all, having obtained eternal redemption.

[194] John 6:54 – Whoever eats My flesh and drinks My blood has eternal life, and I will raise him up at the last day.

Deacon: Amen. Amen. Amen. I believe, I believe, I believe that this is true. Amen. Pray for us and for all Christians who said to us concerning them, "Remember us in the house of the Lord."

The Peace and Love of Jesus Christ be with you. Let us Sing, "Alleluia."

Pray for the worthy communion of the immaculate, heavenly, and Holy Mysteries. Lord have mercy.

Glory to You, O Lord, glory to You.